NEW DIRECTIONS FOR ADULT AND CONTINUING EDUCATION

Susan Imel, *Ohio State University*
EDITOR-IN-CHIEF

⟨ **W9-DCY-641**

The Strategic Use of Learning Technologies

Elizabeth J. Burge
University of New Brunswick

EDITOR

Number 88, Winter 2000

JOSSEY-BASS
San Francisco

#45686737

THE STRATEGIC USE OF LEARNING TECHNOLOGIES
Elizabeth J. Burge (ed.)
New Directions for Adult and Continuing Education, no. 88
Susan Imel, Editor-in-Chief

Microfilm copies of issues and articles are available in 16mm and 35mm, as well as microfiche in 105mm, through University Microfilms Inc., 300 North Zeeb Road, Ann Arbor, Michigan 48106-1346.

ISSN 1052-2891   ISBN 0-7879-5426-8

NEW DIRECTIONS FOR ADULT AND CONTINUING EDUCATION is part of The Jossey-Bass Higher and Adult Education Series and is published quarterly by Jossey-Bass Inc., 350 Sansome Street, San Francisco, California 94104-1342. Periodicals postage paid at San Francisco, California, and at additional mailing offices. Postmaster: Send address changes to New Directions for Adult and Continuing Education, Jossey-Bass Inc., 350 Sansome Street, San Francisco, California 94104-1342.

SUBSCRIPTIONS cost $58.00 for individuals and $104.00 for institutions, agencies, and libraries.

EDITORIAL CORRESPONDENCE should be sent to the Editor-in-Chief, Susan Imel, ERIC/ACVE, 1900 Kenny Road, Columbus, Ohio 43210-1090. E-mail: imel.1@osu.edu.

Cover photograph by Wernher Krutein/PHOTOVAULT © 1990.

www.josseybass.com

Printed in the United States of America on acid-free recycled paper containing 100 percent recovered waste paper, of which at least 20 percent is postconsumer waste.

CONTENTS

EDITOR'S NOTES

Learning technologies: here is a term to unpack, even before we think about how to use these technologies strategically! For this volume, I define a learning technology as any tool that requires informed design and appropriate use in order to enhance an adult's ability to learn; that is, to enhance the use of various information processing strategies and learning activities alone, with peers, and with appropriate advisers and educators. In particular, a learning technology should be as "holistic" a technology as possible— enabling users to exercise maximum control and freedom to create or do what they intend—as distinct from a "prescriptive technology," which calls for compliant and limited responses (Franklin, 1999). If you really think about it, the history of learning technologies is long and the range of technologies vast. Today they include purpose-designed actual and virtual spaces, structured group work, books and journals, audio- and videocassettes, CD-ROMs, programmed learning software, library-based databases, audio, video, and computer conferencing, educational radio, and the Internet. We could step into several terminological tunnels here to unpack all the words in my definition, but I hope that more conceptual light will appear as you browse through the chapters. In this Introduction, you see the reasons for my selection of chapters and the authors' selection of topics they think about in their practice.

A publication that takes a commonsense approach to the use of learning technologies has to go beyond uncritical assumptions about practice, or lengthy technology-specific prescriptions, and focus first on the basic components and dynamics in adult learning situations. I have reflected much on my own thirty years of experience of using conferencing and information delivery technologies, helping adults learn through public and special library services and in other self-directed ways, being a learning designer, moderating professional development activity online and off-line, and now as a higher education faculty member teaching in dual mode (face-to-face and distance simultaneously, using mostly a technology mix of audioconferencing, print, self-study, peer group work, and interaction with experts in course subjects. Frequently, my thoughts revert to fundamental learning tasks such as using a full repertoire of learning strategies, getting fast and tactful academic advice without feeling one is "deficient" or needing a metaphorical crutch to support a weak body, finding and critically using appropriate information sources, knowing how to get the most out of structured discussions, and avoiding feeling annoyed or diminished by dysfunctional technology. There are other matters to consider too in using any learning technology; these include cognitive and psychosocial developmental issues in adulthood, the impact of differences in learning style preferences (not to be confused with learning strategies), the impact of various teaching models, and the equally important factors of gender, age, and ethnicity. But this volume has page limits, so choices had to be made.

A third focus of attention, apart from the learner and learning processes, is how skillfully and consistently I interrogate and understand my practice and how my actions are shaped by the context. When I think about technology, for example, how well do I resist the hyperbole of eager salesfolk or the "quick fix" solutions of poorly informed administrators? How do I place any technology in its historical perspective and see how today's technologies are often transitional? If I decide to ignore sound advice from others about the need for technology mixes (Daniel, 2000), on what basis could I claim intelligent thinking? Am I asking sharp enough questions? (For example, "It may move data, but might its application help move minds?") How could my use of each technology enable me to ensure that learners use all the required learning strategies and not limp along on just a few? How could the inherent features (including strengths and limitations) of any technology be used to accommodate differences in learning style dimensions, or promote reflective or critical thinking? The most challenging question, of course, is this: How do I know if I am asking the right questions?

The authors of this volume have synthesized their practical wisdom to help us think reflectively and strategically about such questions. They keep us focused on learning and learners, for it is they who represent the key issues, not the technology (Gibson, 1998). The authors explain how three well-known technologies may be used for user-centered learning (not an easy concept to practice), and they use their "street smarts" to focus on some future directions for practice. In essence, they help us to keep our balance: to use adult-appropriate learning methods, to avoid being driven by any technology (old or new), to enjoy learning with adults, not to feel pressured to make changes for their own sake, and to be reassured that a blend of the old and the new will always attract adult learners.

Many of the authors refer to open and distance education (ODE) because that field of practice has used many learning technologies over the past one hundred or so years to ensure that adult learners can access well-designed resources and academic advisers and tutors. And all distance educators I know already work in converged modes; that is, their work applies equally to learners who are seen at every class (traditional face-to-face formats) and those who are not seen for every formal encounter with an adviser, a tutor, or a teacher (Tait and Mills, 1999). Not all distance education is open: openness refers to a deliberate institutional policy to give an adult learner opportunities to exercise real (not rhetorical) choice regarding content, entry requirements, content, timing, and academic assessment (see www.open.ac.uk, www.athabascau.ca, and www.nec.org.uk as long-established examples). Do not therefore dismiss what these ODE authors say, because the real point is how to design and manage learning that is relevant to adults. Most of the world's adult distance learners live in cities and towns—distance is usually a financial, scheduling, or psychological issue—

so it is obvious that the walled campus, fixed-time-and-place model of formal education is just not appropriate for many busy adults.

The first three chapters "walk the talk" about putting learners and learning first. They consider why learning strategies play a key role in any designed use of technology, why learner services are so important a series of activities, and why information literacy skills are essential travel skills through the labyrinthine corridors of information resources. Chris Olgren unpacks the concept and functions of learning strategies. She uses her own extensive experience and research to illustrate how teachers (including herself) integrate the full repertoire into learning activities and how learners explain in their own words how they understand the different strategies.

From the U.S.A. to the U.K., we're off to hear Marion Phillips and Patrick Kelly of the United Kingdom's biggest university, The Open University (established in 1969), discuss the rationale and the results of their work in providing learner services. Such exemplary practice demands conceptual skill and years of listening "care-fully" as adults explain the challenges and constraints in integrating academic work into their already busy schedules. You will find no naïve idealism in this chapter: the authors know all the shortcuts that adults (like us) take to get where we need to go, and any educational institution smart enough to realize the relationship between effective learner services and institutional success will enhance its future.

Some readers will note some terminology that is different from theirs; for example, a "tutor" is an academically qualified and specially trained person who works with a small group of learners anywhere in the world (but mostly in the United Kingdom) as each one progresses through course materials designed by a multiskilled team inside The Open University. I have retained such linguistic diversity throughout the volume to pay respect to colleagues in each country.

Then it is back to the United States to see the scope of the knowledge, skills, and attitudes entailed in the concept of information literacy, as outlined by an expert in information seeking and synthesis. Sandra Kerka draws our attention to a concept that I see discussed more often than I see applied in course designs, structured learning activities, or in educators' links with librarians. Being information-literate in general is no mean skill; being thus literate in electronic contexts is quite another (as my own experience as a learner still indicates!).

The fourth chapter takes us to Australia to think about a topic not often discussed frankly in public: the unintended outcomes of using learning technologies. Murphy's Law is not the focus here; the topic is much more complex because the effects over time are unexpected and often not easily visible to either novice or expert practitioner. The laws of technological change operate here, as do various ways to group unintended effects, as Allan Herrmann, Robert Fox, and Anna Boyd explain.

Back to the North American continent now for four chapters that deal with actual learning technologies. I selected three technologies for this section: print, for its enduring ease of use; radio, for its ubiquitous presence; and the

Web for its current impact on how we access and collect information. Jennifer O'Rourke uses her long experience in open and distance education (or *flexible learning,* as it is called in other countries) to remind us of the functions of well-designed print and how they are achieved. To the electronic enthusiasts, print may appear to be just too simple and old-fashioned a technology to command any serious attention (rather as audioconferencing deceives the novice practitioner who cannot yet separate the skills needed to connect the wires from the skills needed to connect the minds). Enhancing the features of print—as we know it at today's level of technical development—requires high levels of skill in interpersonal communication as well as graphical displays of information. Radio likewise is a ubiquitous technology that demands sophisticated knowledge if it is to be effectively integrated into a learner-friendly mix of technologies. The analysis by May Maskow of how a Canadian educational radio station developed innovative and successful programs shows not only her insistence on high-quality teaching but also her healthy respect for the essence of this medium—when used skillfully it renders the speakers psychologically present in a unique way.

The Web commands much attention now even though it is still in early stages of development, so here we have two opportunities for reflection. One is to get behind the screen to see how a savvy professional developer thinks about her work—which may be likened at times to walking on eggshells. Genevieve Gallant has experience helping teachers who are either resisting change because of workload stress or other factors, or resisting everyday realities while under the seductive spell of technological promises. The second opportunity is to stay on-screen with Brent Wilson and May Lowry as they learn constructively and typically using the Web's resources. You may need time off from work to explore all the Web sites they offer! This time factor is one of the points they raise and it leads us back to the information-seeking and processing issues outlined earlier by Sandra Kerka and Chris Olgren.

After this fast trip through a complex but challenging landscape, you have an opportunity to think synthetically in the final chapter. How far does anything you have read resonate with your own values, experience, learning interests, and goals? Has our collection of reflections helped you to think constructively—that is, to act as your own information architect but guided by colleagues?

Read on.

Elizabeth J. Burge
Editor

References

Daniel, J. D. "The Internet and Higher Education: Preparing for Change." Address to the Internet Revolution Conference, London, United Kingdom, May 9, 2000. [www.open.ac.uk/vcs-speeches/IntEdRev.html]

Franklin, U. *The Real World of Technology* (2nd ed.). Toronto, Ontario: House of Anansi Press, 1999.

Gibson, C. C. (ed.). *Distance Learners in Higher Education: Institutional Responses for Quality Outcomes*. Madison, Wis.: Atwood Publishing, 1998.

Tait, A., and Mills, R. (eds.) *The Convergence of Distance and Conventional Education: Patterns of Flexibility for the Individual Learner*. London: Routledge, 1999.

ELIZABETH J. BURGE, a guest professor at Mid Sweden University for 2000–2001, is professor of adult education and distance education at the University of New Brunswick in Atlantic Canada.

1

A review of learning strategies shows why it is necessary to take a learner-centered view before thinking about technology.

Learning Strategies for Learning Technologies

Christine H. Olgren

Using technology for education and training offers many challenges, but perhaps the greatest is to focus not on the technology itself but on the learner and learning. Technology invites a tools-first emphasis, but technology is only as good as our knowledge of how to use it to enhance learning.

In teaching and designing for technology-assisted learning, I continually remind myself to begin with the learner. For one, doing that keeps me grounded in the learner's shoes or what it would be like to be a learner in my course. For another, it helps me to cast a critical eye on what is likely to work and not work to foster effective outcomes.

So I share with you some thoughts from the learner's viewpoint. Adopting this view helps me to see better how people learn with technology and what strategies they use to learn. Insights gained from the learner can help answer five key questions: What is different about learning with technology? What concepts help us to understand the learning process? What kinds of learning strategies do adults use? How do we connect learning strategies with learning technologies? And what are some future directions from a learning viewpoint?

What Is Different About Learning with Technology?

Learning with technology is usually characterized by a physical separation between learner and instructor and by the use of media for communications and content resources. Those characteristics have important effects on the learner. First, learners have more autonomy and responsibility for carrying out the learning process. Second, learners must be able to use technology to access resources and communicate with others. Third, learners may find it more difficult to determine expectations and to remain motivated when there is less direct contact with an instructor or other students.

How learners respond to such conditions and are helped to manage them are critical factors not only for their persistence in completing a course but also for the quality of their learning outcomes. To gain insights into how people learn with technology and the kinds of skills they need, let us take a closer look at the learning process from the learner's perspective.

What Concepts Help Us to Understand the Learning Process?

The axiom "begin with the learner" seems a simple and obvious starting point. However, applying it in practice may lead to being mired in sinking sands without a solid footpath. An organizing framework is needed. Each individual is complex and unique and enters into a learning experience with a variety of backgrounds, attitudes, skills, and motivations. What do we need to know about learners and how they learn? What concepts contribute to an organizing framework of guiding principles? My key concepts are *learning strategies, goals, motivations, relevance,* and *outcomes.*

The concept of learning strategies is very powerful in understanding how people learn because it focuses attention on what people do to manage the learning process and construct knowledge in memory; how goals, motivations, perceptions, and skills affect learning; and why differences in learning strategies lead to differences in learning outcomes.

Learning strategies are defined as thoughts and behaviors engaged in by the learner in order to accomplish goals or purposes. That is, the strategies are intended to affect how people learn, think, and motivate themselves in order to carry out a learning task. Weinstein and Hume (1998, p. 11) capture the essence of a learning strategy well: "learning with skill, will, and self-regulation." A capable learner has the skills to learn successfully, the will or desire to use those skills, and the ability to manage the learning process.

If you analyzed learning strategies, you'd find four elements: a goal, skills, perceptions, and motivational influences. Learning strategies are directed to accomplishing a goal or purpose, employ relevant thinking and learning skills to achieve the goal, and are influenced by the learner's perceptions of the task and intrinsic or extrinsic motivations to learn. You would also find various types of learning strategies, but most fall into three general categories: cognitive strategies for mentally processing information, metacognitive strategies for planning and managing the learning process, and affective strategies for maintaining motivation and psychological readiness.

Are learning strategies the same thing as learning styles? No. There are important differences between the two. A learning strategy is situational and will differ in relation to different goals and motivations. In contrast, learning styles are defined as learning behaviors that are relatively stable and employed with some consistency across different kinds of situations (James and Blank, 1993). You might say a strategy is like a plan of action, whereas a style is like a preferred way of acting. Learners use certain strategies to accomplish goals. Learners use certain styles because it is how they like to learn.

Perhaps two vignettes will help to illustrate the important connection between strategies and motivations, and in turn, outcomes. Both of these learners were enrolled in an undergraduate course in marketing and were working toward a bachelor's degree via distance education.

The case of Dave: Dave is a manager at a manufacturing plant. He was recently promoted on the condition that he finish his bachelor's degree. Dave admits that his only reason for enrolling in the marketing course is that his employer requires him to get a degree. There's nothing, he says, he wants to learn for himself, although part of his job involves sales. He believes that most academic learning does not relate to real life. With a family and long hours at work, he wants to spend the least amount of time possible to get a decent grade. Dave develops what might be called a "management strategy" that emphasizes the efficient use of time, effort, and resources. The strategy is directed to his goals of completing the course quickly and conveniently. In planning his strategy, Dave decides to make an audiocassette for each course module. He can save time by listening to the tapes while driving to and from work. Dave sees his car as a quiet and convenient place to concentrate. Rather than read everything, Dave skims the modules to find the major topics. He organizes the topics into an outline, summarizes important concepts, and finds a few examples. He then records the information on tape. He listens to the tape one or two times until he feels he knows the material well enough to get a passing grade on the exam. At the end of the marketing course, Dave said he didn't learn anything of value but he completed it with little disruption to his work or family life. Dave's strategies, then, reflect choices he made to minimize his time and effort.

The case of Jane: Jane is the manager of a small grocery store. Jane's reasons for getting a degree are to improve her work skills and get a better job. Her goals in the marketing course are to find practical ideas she can use in her work, particularly sales promotion and fundraising, and to do well on the exam. Jane says she's a practical person who likes to develop procedures to guide her work. She's also a busy person, so she creates brief learning spaces whenever she can throughout the day. Fortunately, she has good concentration and can read almost anyplace. Jane develops a "practical strategy" that balances her personal goals with course requirements. She first skims the material to get an overview of the content and scope of the task. She then devises a general plan about what she wants to learn for herself, what the instructor requires, and how much time it will take. In her reading, Jane is mentally involved in understanding the content and applying it to her work. She highlights major points in her mind, looks for relationships among concepts, and builds a mental outline to organize the material. She also relates the material to her own experience, and she pauses frequently to reflect about their usefulness. At the end of the course, Jane found she had gained many practical ideas that she incorporated into her job, and she got a good grade. She discovered unanticipated outcomes: she felt she grew as a person and she opened up to new possibilities in her work. She also learned how to market herself in job interviews.

As Dave and Jane illustrate, different goals lead to different strategies. In turn, different strategies lead to different learning outcomes. Dave's goals of minimizing time and effort to pass an exam and earn a degree are prime examples of extrinsic motivation in doing only what is required to complete a task. He employed efficient management strategies, but his mental engagement in learning the content was superficial. The resulting outcome was that he learned very little. Jane's goals, in contrast, demonstrated an intrinsic motivation to learn the content itself to improve work skills and to find new ideas to apply on the job. She used a variety of strategies to process the content actively: highlighting main ideas in her mind, looking for relationships between concepts, building a mental outline to organize topics, relating the material to examples from her own experience, and pausing to mentally apply ideas to her work. As a result of such active mental engagement, Jane understood the material well and integrated it with her own experience and applications.

What Kinds of Learning Strategies Do Adults Use?

Viewed as a whole, and exemplified by the cases of Dave and Jane, we can see how strategies work together to help the learner accomplish goals. Let us go the next step and pick these strategies apart to see what else they tell us.

If we ask learners directly how they learn, they will describe various kinds of learning strategies (Olgren, 1998; Burge, 1994; Eastmond, 1995; Marton, Hounsell, and Entwistle, 1997). The strategies can be categorized into four types, with each type directed to a different aspect of the overall learning process:

Orientation Strategies. Becoming oriented to the learning experience is a crucial first stage in preparing to learn. Students gauge their comfort level with the technology, identify required tasks, appraise the course's value or usefulness, establish goals or a purpose for learning, estimate time and effort, and make an informal plan about how to proceed.

Management Strategies. Because learning with technology gives learners more autonomy and responsibility, they need management strategies for directing the learning process. Such strategies include monitoring comprehension, managing time and pacing, staying on track, maintaining motivation, persisting to completion, using resources, and seeking help when needed.

Information Processing Strategies. Learners construct knowledge in memory through various strategies for processing information, often called *cognitive strategies*. Learners apply thinking skills to learn the subject matter. I like to think of this as mental engagement in learning, where learners interact with the content by using various strategies for selecting, organizing, and integrating information. Cognitive strategies directly affect the outcomes of how well learners are able to remember, understand, and apply the material.

Evaluation of Learning Outcomes. Because most education programs emphasize evaluation from an instructional viewpoint, it is easy to overlook the extent to which learners engage in self-evaluating outcomes. Self-evaluation strategies are commonly used by learners to assess their readiness for exams or to determine what they learned, the new knowledge or skills they gained, and if their goals were met. Although self-evaluation is part of knowing how to learn in any setting, it is especially important in learning with technology, where feedback is less immediate.

If we compare the four types of strategies, we find that many are metacognitive. Becoming oriented, managing the learning process, and evaluating outcomes all require metacognitive strategies in knowing how to plan, regulate, and assess learning. As learners said in an online course I teach, the most important skills in learning with technology are self-direction, self-discipline, self-motivation, time management, taking initiative, staying on track, and skills in organizing resources. A recent study found that distance learners reported four times the use of metacognitive strategies compared with classroom learners. In addition, the two groups used different types of metacognitive strategies; self-management was used most often by distance learners but accounted for a low proportion of the strategies used by classroom learners (White, 1999). Similar findings were reported by Olgren (1998), Burge (1994), and Eastmond (1995).

How Do We Connect Learning Strategies with Learning Technologies?

The learners' own stories about how they learn tell me a great deal about how to teach and design with technology. I use their learning strategies to generate guiding principles about the components to include in course designs. My aim is to link learning strategies to learning technologies by providing design components that activate, mirror, and support strategies for effective learning.

I find the following six guiding principles to be most important because my goal as an adult educator is to trigger intrinsic motivation and provide a clear structure that supports learning through technology:

• Provide well-crafted orientation materials to create comfort in using technology and to trigger planning strategies for how to approach the course.

- Have learners articulate their intrinsic goals for learning and help them to find the relevance by making connections between the materials and their own needs, interests, and applications.
- Provide a course structure that is divided into manageable chunks, where each segment has a content overview, practical examples, application guidelines, one or more activities, and clear directions about what to do.
- Design interactive learning activities that engage learners in clearly specified tasks involving analysis, synthesis, application, or evaluation of concepts situated in real or simulated settings.
- Include one or more activities in which learners self-evaluate their learning by comparing outcomes to goals, identifying important ideas gained, and identifying improvements to be made.
- Ensure that any technology used is as transparent as possible so that the learner's energies remain focused on learning and not on operating the equipment.

Orientation Materials. I put a great deal of time into developing orientation materials because I want to make sure students begin their work with positive perceptions and intrinsic motivations. I also view orientation materials as a springboard to help learners formulate strategies about how to proceed.

Here is what three different learners say about orienting strategies: (1) "I try to get some practice with the technology before the course starts so I feel comfortable and don't worry about that aspect." (2) "When I start a new course the first thing I do is look for where the instructor is coming from. I want to know what she thinks about the subject and what I'm required to do. Then I'll glance at the material to see how much I already know and what I might be interested in. That helps me to determine what to learn and my goals." (3) "Before I even start a course, I look over the materials to get an idea of how I want to attack it. Then I develop a 'semi-plan' of what I'm going to do and how much time and effort I'll put in."

We often underestimate the importance of this preparation phase. Although most courses provide some form of syllabus or orientation, they may not include enough information to help learners to feel comfortable with the technology and to relate the content to their own intrinsic purposes for learning. As a result, they may choose strategies just to "get by" or they may not become invested enough in the course to complete it.

In course orientations I clearly state requirements and expectations, provide content overviews with a personal touch about my own perspective, include examples of how the content is relevant to real-world situations and applications, and provide planning cues or activities. In technology orientations I include practice activities with step-by-step directions about how to use each tool; for example, how to post messages and navigate Web-based discussion forums. I also provide students with tips and skill-development exercises for improving their learning strategies.

Learning Goals. It is important to determine goals for learning for several reasons. Goals help to situate learning in a learner's own context of needs, interests, or applications; articulate intrinsic motivations to learn; identify relevant material to emphasize; provide a "touchstone" to monitor progress and keep on track; and provide a means for evaluating the outcomes of learning. Goals are also the basis for developing learning strategies.

Here is what three different learners say about goals: (1) "Establishing my own goals or objectives is essential for making decisions about where to focus attention and what to learn as well as keeping on track or having purpose and direction." (2) "I found I have to have some goals to focus my learning and to stick with it." (3) "I always think about what I'm interested in learning. My own interest really helps me to concentrate and learn. If it's something that interests you, you're more motivated to ask additional questions to find out even more information."

As educators we commonly state a course's instructional objectives, but we are far less likely to ask learners about their goals. For adults, who are pragmatic about what they want to learn, goals are an important motivator in finding useful ideas and maintaining persistence. At the start of a course, I always ask learners to state three or four goals they have in relation to their interests, needs, and applications. I also ask them to revisit their goals periodically throughout a course in order to monitor progress and potential changes.

Course Structure. Well-structured course materials are particularly important in learning with technology because they support and trigger learners' strategies for managing the learning process. As one student said, "Being a distance learner has helped to highlight the importance of having a good structure to follow of clearly written instructions and activities that help me to pace myself and manage time." Time management can be difficult for adults who have to juggle the conflicting demands of work or family responsibilities and for whom there is no clear division between learning space and work or family space, as there is in a classroom.

Here is what four different learners say about management strategies: (1) "I've learned how to manage my time better, and I now set up a regular hour every morning to log into my course to read messages so I don't get overwhelmed." (2) "It's important for me to set a timetable about when to start and complete each module. Otherwise I procrastinate." (3) "It's easy to go off on tangents when there are lots of resources, like Web links. Then I have to go back to what's required or my own goals to get back on task." (4) "Sometimes I find myself highlighting almost everything. Then I need to stop and think, 'What am I doing here, what's my purpose?'"

In structuring a course, I divide it into weekly segments and divide materials into manageable units that can be completed in one- or two-hour blocks. Each segment includes a content overview, examples, familiar analogies, application guidelines, one or more learning activities, and clear explanations of what to do and when. A clear structure, then, helps to offset the effects of technology by serving as a communications bridge between instructor and learner. However, clarity does not mean inflexibility. To support learners in meeting their own intrinsic goals, I always provide some flexibility in how students respond to the activities and which resource materials they emphasize.

Learning Activities. My approach to designing learning activities uses technology to cue and support learners' cognitive strategies. I think of these activities as having two purposes: to achieve an outcome in learning some aspect of the subject matter, and to trigger cognitive strategies that involve analysis, synthesis, evaluation, or application of information. The two purposes go hand-in-hand because cognitive processes are intimately connected to learning outcomes. In other words, how you learn determines what you learn.

Here is what five different learners say about cognitive strategies: (1) "The biggest thing I do is relate the material to something I know. That really helps me to understand and remember it. When I'm reading, I'm always thinking about how something I've done in the past relates to this. Then, I'll stop and think about it before continuing on." (2) "I try to relate what I'm learning to things I see in the newspapers, magazines, or watching TV. If I can apply it, I'll remember it." (3) "I observe my coworkers to see if what they do fits with what I'm learning. Sometimes I'll stop reading and role-play how I'd apply it at work." (4) "I like to break things up into parts and analyze how they work. I even draw charts to understand categories and subcategories. If I put things into a matrix, then I know I understand how they work." (5) "While I'm reading I'm asking myself questions, 'What's this about? How does it work? What do I know about this?'"

As the learners suggest, active engagement in learning involves mentally interacting with the content and relating it to prior knowledge and applications. Activities that stimulate their cognitive strategies include case studies, scenarios, role-plays, debates, miniprojects, problem exercises, or journals that situate learning in real-world or simulated contexts. In technology-assisted learning, those types of activities add important learner-to-content or learner-to-learner interactions where students interact directly with resource materials or with each other to carry out the activities.

Evaluation. Involving learners in self-evaluation is an important part of the overall teaching-learning process. Although I provide feedback from an instructional perspective, I believe that learning is most valuable when students can see for themselves how the learning experience has changed their knowledge, skills, attitudes, or work applications. Engaging in self-assessment also helps learners to gain skills in taking responsibility for learning and identifying outcomes relevant to them.

Here is what three different learners say: (1) "After I'm done with a course, I review things in my mind. I ask myself, 'What did I learn? Do I understand how things work?'" (2) "Anytime I can read with more understanding or assess with more understanding something that's going on today, then I think I've learned that out of the courses I'm taking." (3) "I look at how the information changed my way of doing things, how I look at something, how I understand something. I know I've learned something if it becomes part of how I look at things and do things."

To build self-evaluation into a course, I use activities that ask learners to identify three or four important things they learned and to explain why those outcomes were important to them. I also ask them to compare the outcomes to their initial goals for the course to see if their goals were met, why or why not, and if unanticipated discoveries were made. Just as course beginnings should involve an assessment of goals, course endings should involve an assessment of outcomes to help learners reflect on and integrate what they have learned.

What Are Some Future Directions from a Learning Viewpoint?

I've sketched out briefly some ideas about how learning strategies can be incorporated into course designs to create technology environments that support engaged learning. Tapping the full potential of learning strategies to inform course design decisions is increasingly important for two reasons. The first is the ongoing development of interactive multimedia technology. Educational technology is continually adding new tools and capabilities for interactive multimedia formats. More technology options create more complexity in knowing when to use text, graphics, audio, video, synchronous, or asynchronous formats. Knowledge about how people learn from different media can provide important insights to guide media selection and design decisions. Such knowledge can also help create technology environments that engage the learner in an active process of knowledge development rather than distract the learner with equipment operations. The second reason is greater student diversity. As the use of technology-assisted learning expands to new audiences, adult learners as a whole are increasingly more diverse in age, backgrounds, life experiences, culture, learning skills, and other characteristics. We need to understand how differences in student characteristics affect learning strategies so that course designs are both appropriate and supportive. Knowledge about differences in learning strategies is also important for helping students to develop their skills in knowing how to learn with technology.

Adopting a learning perspective invites us to rethink the roles of technology and teaching. The role of technology is not to be a delivery system but rather to be an environment that enables learning. The role of teaching is not simply to convey information but rather to engage students in actively constructing knowledge. The challenge of teaching with technology is to create a learning design that cues and supports the full repertoire of learning strategies.

References

Burge, E. J. "Learning in Computer Conference Contexts: The Learners' Perspective." *Journal of Distance Education,* 1994, *9*(1), 19–43.

Eastmond, D. V. *Alone But Together: Adult Distance Study by Computer Conferencing.* Cresskill, N.J.: Hampton Press, 1995.

James, W. B., and Blank, W. E. "Review and Critique of Available Learning Style Instruments for Adults." In D. D. Flannery (ed.), *Applying Cognitive Learning Theory to Adult Learning.* New Directions for Adult and Continuing Education, no. 59. San Francisco: Jossey-Bass, 1993.

Marton, F., Hounsell, D., and Entwistle, N. *The Experience of Learning.* Edinburgh: Scottish Academic Press, 1997.

Olgren, C. H. "Improving Learning Outcomes: The Effects of Learning Strategies and Motivations." In C. C. Gibson (ed.), *Distance Learners in Higher Education: Institutional Responses for Quality Outcomes.* Madison, Wis.: Atwood Publishing, 1998.

Weinstein, C. E., and Hume, L. M. *Study Strategies for Lifelong Learning.* Washington, D.C: American Psychological Association, 1998.

White, C. J. "The Metacognitive Knowledge of Distance Learners." *Open Learning,* 1999, *14*(3), 37–46.

CHRISTINE H. OLGREN *is program director of the Distance Education Professional Development Program at the University of Wisconsin-Madison.*

2

Information technology can be helpful in supporting advice, guidance, and student learning services, but its successful use demands constant attention to learners' realities and a skeptical enthusiast's attitude.

Learning Technologies for Learner Services

Marion Phillips, Patrick Kelly

A service for adult learners that complements the core teaching process and offers advice and guidance to help students to learn effectively is an integral component of successful open and distance education (ODE). Such a service is especially important in technology-mediated contexts for five important reasons:

- The learners are usually mature adults, studying on a part-time basis. They need educational and organizational skills to save their time and money and to maintain a balance between the often-competing demands of study, family, friends, work, and social life.
- Usually, the open learner is physically separated both from the teacher and fellow students for much of the time.
- Adult learners do not just need to revive "rusty" study skills; most need to develop a whole new set of learning and information literacy strategies.
- Learners in ODE systems are often not subject to admission criteria that demand prior educational qualifications. This openness is a particular canon of The Open University (OU) in the United Kingdom, so our continuing challenge is to offer undergraduate courses comparable in quality to other universities, but without imposing academic entrance requirements of any kind and without merely offering learners a chance to fail (see www.open.ac.uk).
- ODE is usually very flexible with students having a high degree of choice. Our students can choose single courses or group their course credits together for specific qualifications such as undergraduate or postgraduate certificates, diplomas, and degrees. Such an open curriculum allows

undergraduate students the freedom to construct a study program of interest or relevance without the constraint of subject or faculty boundaries. Students can take a degree in a named subject area but there is no compulsion to do so; they may choose courses in any order, at any level, and from any faculty they wish.

What Is a Learner Service?

These five factors—competing life demands, physical separation, learning skill needs, open admission policy, and program-course choice flexibility—create specific demands for focused and timely support for learners. We manage the provision of this support and the mediating effects of each applied learning technology. We do not necessarily mirror what happens in traditional settings, nor does technology mediation always create helpful effects. Let us explain.

For us, a learner service is not just giving initial advice for inquirers or dealing with student problems, nor is it just the responsibility of a small group of specialized counseling staff. Advice, guidance, and study support are developmental factors in the whole learning process and include activities such as choosing and planning a study program, organizing study, developing learning skills, monitoring progress, and managing university procedures. Also, students should be able to access advice and guidance as they need to, including career guidance and special needs facilities.

All these learning needs are explicitly related to the four principal phases of the student career: entry, induction, on course–on program, and completion–moving on. Bailey, Brown, and Kelly (1996) see these phases and their related objectives as generic, although the provision and method of delivery will vary from institution to institution.

What Is Provided and Why?

During the first, or entry, phase of a student's career, from initial inquiry to enrollment, the learner service can provide useful information and access to advice and guidance so that the adult learner may make an informed choice about the decision to study, the selection of courses, and the program of study. The information includes descriptions of courses and qualifications available, admissions policies, fees, information about student services, and sources of further advice. Advisory staff offer guidance and advice to enable learners to make an informed choice; inquirers are invited to open meetings and can request or may be sent diagnostic materials and information about opportunities to prepare for learning.

The second phase involves induction into the university. In addition to introducing the university's operations and the mode of open learning, a learner service helps adults develop learning and student skills for successful transition into higher education. The service might include giving out orientation and preparatory material and ensuring an opportunity for adults to attend an introductory meeting with their personal tutor. (A *tutor* is an academically qualified and specially trained person who works with a small group of learners anywhere in the world—but mostly in the United Kingdom—as each one progresses through course materials designed by a multiskilled team inside The Open University.)

As the learner progresses through the course or qualification (the third phase), the tutor will be responsible for immediate on-course academic support, including feedback on assignments, tutorial support, monitoring student progress, and acting as a point of first contact for the student's queries. Nevertheless, Brindley (1995) affirms that there is still much specialist guidance and study support that can be provided by the learner service to meet specific learners' needs—for example, learning and study skills workshops, services for disabled students, guidance on future course choice, professional recognition and careers, and help with administrative and operational matters.

Finally, as a student completes a course or qualification and prepares to move on (fourth phase), the learner service can provide information, advice, and guidance about further study options and career opportunities, academic transcripts, and references and recognition of achievement.

Historically, learner services have been the poor cousin of teaching and therefore vulnerable to reductions in times of budget constraints. However, there is now much greater awareness that advice, guidance, and student services can give institutions a marketing edge and help increase retention and the overall quality of the learning experience. The U.K. government–backed system of quality assurance for higher education includes student support and guidance as one of the six core aspects of provision to be assessed (Quality Assurance Agency, 2000).

Which Learning Technologies Are Used?

A holistic learner service can be mediated through a variety of learning technologies ranging from simple printed guides and other written materials to complex interactive electronic systems. Similarly, advisory staff can offer guidance and advice by letter, telephone, and face-to-face meetings as well as by using the new technologies. So how can we choose which learning technologies to use to provide an effective and accessible learner service for our students?

One of the hallmarks of ODE is the use of a wide variety of teaching media ranging from print to television and video, radio and audiocassettes, and increasingly, information and communication technologies (ICT). The OU uses a multimedia approach to learner services: initially these were based on face-to-face contact, the telephone, and written materials, but now they have been expanded to include e-mail, computer conferencing, and the Internet. We own up here to being two skeptical enthusiasts as we develop

Web-based advice, guidance, and learner services for inquirers and students (Phillips, Scott, and Fage, 1998). Although our student response is positive and there is huge potential for further enhancement, we have no illusions; we are at the "just-starting-to-crawl" stage and do not expect to be walking for some time. It is worth noting, amid all the hype, that the Web has been with us for little more than a decade and there is still much to learn in using it. Almost every educational institution has a Web site but we are depressed by the number that serve no discernible purpose other than to announce, "Hey, we have a Web site."

As the new technologies affect learner advice and support, this process raises the question of whether the increasing use of ICT is likely to sweep away current tried-and-true practices. Students are certainly making use of the new media for studying. For example, at the time of writing, the OU Web site receives approximately five hundred thousand page hits a week, a quarter of our courses require a personal computer, and forty thousand of our students are online. These numbers grow rapidly.

At the same time, students also increasingly use the telephone to contact our learner service—to the extent of 1,500,000 calls annually from inquirers and enrolled students. In addition, our work and our reputation relies on well-designed printed materials; for our learner service, these products include, for example, brochures that describe the university's courses and teaching system, preparatory and learning skills resources, administrative information, and careers materials.

We still offer printed materials for several reasons. At least for now, a reasonable number of our students report no or very limited access to a computer with Internet link. Also, we do not assume that all our students will have the appropriate skills for using these new electronic media, or the finance to support their online costs. In addition, although we are beginning to experiment with multimedia, many of our Web resources are derived from existing printed documents and materials and students may well prefer to study by reading from paper rather than sitting in front of a screen for long periods of time. We continue to offer individual contact at a distance via the telephone, because we know that this technology is still a preferred medium for many adult learners.

Nevertheless, as more and more students need access to computers for study, they expect to be able to access learner services and the university's administration through these media. Even in courses where computers are not required, a growing number of students and tutors communicate by e-mail. Ignoring the new learning technologies is not an option, but our approach is to use them appropriately alongside traditional teaching and learning media. As a result, the need to provide resources in a variety of media is likely to increase costs rather than reduce them, at least in the short term and possibly for much longer. Our concern is whether students will feel that significant study costs are being transferred to them. For their course fee they used to receive well-designed teaching materials; now they need to buy a PC to participate in the course and spend a small fortune printing hard copy in order to avoid eyestrain. There is also the question of whether institutions are ready for the additional tuition costs, which are expected because the tutor is likely to spend more time online. Many students are reluctant to interrupt their tutor with a phone call but few have any inhibitions about sending e-mails. The telephone conversation between tutor and student is a private affair, but the e-mail exchange is semipublic. As a result, the tutor has to construct the response carefully—in effect to prepare a mini-tutorial—because even if he or she doesn't forward the reply to a study problem to the rest of the group, the student who received it probably will. The face-to-face tutorial has a fixed cost, and the number of tutorials can be controlled. In comparison, e-mail contact is potentially open-ended and the more helpful the tutor is the greater the demand and cost will be.

ICT and Learner Services

Information and communication technologies (ICT) are already being used in various ways to support adult learning (Kirkwood, 1998; Vincent and Whalley, 1998). Information, advice, and therapy services are offered over the Internet: Offer (1993) discusses the increasing use of the Web for career guidance; King, Engi, and Poulis (1998) outline the use of ICT to assist family therapy; Sampson, Kolodinsky, and Greeno (1997), Tait (1999), and Murphy and Mitchell (1998) describe Internet-based counseling services, and Scott, Curson, Shipton, and McAuley (1996) have produced a counseling information support system for university students.

However, such use of the Web has raised concerns among some practitioners who fear that human relations will be "mechanized" through the use of ICT. Written words can be misinterpreted: the clues from nonverbal behavior are absent and it may not be possible to communicate warmth and caring through computer-mediated communication (Watts, 1996). Some are also concerned about the potential loss of confidentiality because hackers can break into material on the Web.

Electronic media are starting to make a significant contribution to learner services. In the process they are helping to improve the relationship between the individual student and the educational institution by enabling students to become active members of a learning community with easy access to fellow students and their tutor, and links to other staff and to student societies. ICT can improve efficiency, and more importantly for an effective learner service, they may enable ODE institutions to personalize their support systems by providing the mechanism for closer links between the student and the institution. At present or shortly our students will have access online to their personal records and to information and advice about their progress for their course and qualification. They will be able to register and pay fees, undertake preparatory work, and receive an induction to study, access university information, communicate with their tutor and student group, access course materials and learning skills resources, send assignments, and take exams.

Smart applications of the new media will eventually provide a learner service that both fulfills all the generic functions and relates to the needs and life contexts of each adult learner. The use, for example, of hyperlinks and online searching facilities can help students access information and guidance opportunities as and when they need to. In addition, online interactive exercises and Internet multimedia can help to make adult learning issues come alive (Scott and Phillips, 1998). We contend that the provision of learner support through ICT will become an indispensable part of advice and guidance services. The use of ICT in the provision of learner advice and support services does not make personal support with real people redundant. In our experience, students do not want to be asked to choose between traditional methods and the new electronic media. They want whatever works best for them.

Offering online learner services can often increase students' understanding of the issues confronting them and also save their time and money. For example, the student is better informed before entering into discussion with learning support staff. But it is still possible, through poor planning of online navigation, to get the balance wrong and cause media and information overload. The student enrolls because of an interest in literature or chemistry but spends time failing to master the mix of print, audiovisual, computer, and Internet learning technologies and gives up in despair without ever really engaging with the content of the course.

Course Choice and Study Planning: An Example

To increase learners' sense of competence in choosing courses and a program, we develop ICT for learner support in three main areas: the provision of information, carrying out business transactions, and learner services.

At its simplest, ICT can be used to provide an online brochure containing details of the various courses offered by the institution. A more complex system may allow online enrollment and other administrative transactions. However, a *real service* for students will also involve opportunities for learner advice and support.

Because we can anticipate from experience many of the questions that the online user might raise, we have produced generic resources available on the OU Web site, mainly in the form of simple html text (www.open. ac.uk/learners-guide).

The *Learner's Guide to The Open University* contains detailed background information about what studying with the OU involves, how supported open learning works, study time requirements, the significance of various academic levels, study preparation options, credit transfer, residential schools, special needs, and the role of the tutor. A series of case studies of "typical students" shows what it is really like to study with the OU. Both new and continuing students need guidance about their choice of course because at undergraduate level there are no entry requirements for any of the 150 or so courses available. Some courses can be combined into prescribed qualifications—for example, named diplomas and B.A. and B.S. degrees—and all students have the option to "pick and mix" various courses into a package that leads to an "open" degree.

For an online guidance system to be useful, it is essential that students be able to access information as and when required—they are unlikely to want to work their way through a whole book of advice! We try to achieve this efficiently by providing many clear navigation links between our resources and other sections of the OU Web site. For example, an inquirer scanning the online course brochure might dip into the *Learner's Guide* to learn what is meant by a level 1 or a level 3 course, or what regional services are available.

The *Learner's Guide* encourages users to think through making choices, to seek information, and to explore key issues. It is also designed to be interactive. One example is our time management exercise. It has proved very difficult to convey in print the reality of the hours needed for undergraduate-level work. Many students who withdraw from courses say they underestimated the amount of time required; a written paper note about time management (along with other allegedly helpful advisory jewels) can all too easily be thought banal and cheerfully ignored by a busy adult. We need to help inquirers fully understand the time demands they will face before they commit themselves. The time management exercise asks prospective students to assess how much time they will have available and what other life tasks they will have to give up in order to find the necessary hours for study. The computer adds up the time the students can allocate and then offers advice about whether this is sufficient to complete a course successfully. Three versions of the exercise are offered to take account of differing computer specifications: a fully interactive version with audio advice, a similar version with text-based advice (for those who cannot or do not wish to hear the audio), and an html text version for the user to download and complete off-line. The *Learner's Guide* is part of the OU provision, but it functions as a reality check more than a marketing tool, and we are committed to helping the learner make informed choices.

Course choice and study planning is only one small part of our online service. We include resources for career guidance, for students with disabilities, detailed preparation for study, induction into the university, how to manage the university (context management to help the learner feel in control), and learning and study skill development. Each of these areas of the *Learner's Guide* will contain information, advice, and guidance opportunities and interactive exercises.

The Future

In developing our strategy for online learner services we do not intend to replace the current service. Rather, we want to provide an additional service that exploits the new media and responds to the growing numbers of adults who use it already. The *Learner's Guide,* for example, prompts users to contact real advisers if further information or guidance is needed; it facilitates such an exchange through e-mail and provides telephone contact numbers. We also plan to offer real-time online access to advisers in the future.

However, it would be foolish to ignore concerns about costs or worries about the ultimate direction of ICT developments. The cost of gaining access to a computer with an Internet link often falls directly on the individual student, and inevitably, it will be a barrier to study for some people. The era of the digitally dispossessed has arrived. This is a particular issue for institutions that have a mission to widen participation. The OU would lose credibility if it did not use the new media, but at present fewer than half the homes in the United Kingdom have an Internet-linked PC. If, as seems probable, access becomes commonplace as a result of a fusion of television and computing technologies, then ICT has real potential to transform ODE by enabling learners to use a much wider range of resources and become active members of a learning community with easy links to their tutor and fellow students.

It is difficult to predict if the virtual institution will ever occupy more than a niche market or if is destined to become the mainstream. Our experience suggests taking a cautious approach. Recent research studies indicate that our adult OU students assume that the university will make greater use of ICT for teaching and learner support. They expect to be able to telephone the university in the evening and over the weekend. They value correspondence tuition. They want some opportunities for face-to-face tutorial contact. They like the flexibility of e-mail communication with their tutor and fellow students. It is also clear that students—our paying customers—fear the university plans to expand computer conferencing (which is not highly regarded) at the expense of face-to-face support (which is). They have also voiced concerns about the possibility that the OU might move away from more personal forms of contact toward more remote services delivered electronically. "For the online and Net-sophisticated respondents, e-mail had rapidly become their preferred method of contacting the OU for both administration and tutors. Net-naïve students believed that e-mailing the OU would become their main method of contact in the future but worried that the OU may go ahead with exclusive e-mail contact and that they would be left behind" (Open University, 2000).

Some argue that the next generation of students who have grown up with computers, Nintendos, Playstations, e-mail, and the Internet will be different from their predecessors. We are not so sure. In the United Kingdom, both primary (five to eleven age group) and secondary schools (eleven to eighteen age group) use ICT as an *additional* resource, not as a replacement for the classroom, library, books, or interaction with the teacher or other pupils. This strategy could mean that the next generation of adult ODE students also will expect to use all the learning technologies. This expectation may be the real challenge for adult educators everywhere.

References

Bailey, D., Brown, J., and Kelly, P. "Academic Advice, Personal Counselling, and On-Programme Guidance in the Open University." In *Personal Tutoring and Academic Advice in Focus,* Paper DQE 224. London: Higher Education Quality Council, 1996. [www.niss.ac.uk/education/heqc/pubs.html]

Brindley, J. "Learners and Learner Services: The Key to the Future in Open Distance Learning." In J. M. Roberts and E. M. Keough (eds.), *Why the Information Highway? Lessons from Open and Distance Learning.* Toronto: Trifolium Books, 1995.

King, S. A., Engi, S., and Poulis, S. T. "Using the Internet to Assist Family Therapy." *British Journal of Guidance and Counselling,* 1998, 26(1), 43–52.

Kirkwood, A. "New Media Mania: Can Information and Communication Technologies Enhance the Quality of Open and Distance Learning?" *Distance Education,* 1998, 19(2), 228–241.

Murphy, L. J., and Mitchell, D. l. "When Writing Helps to Heal: E-mail as Therapy." *British Journal of Guidance and Counselling,* 1998, 26(1), 21–31.

Offer, M. "The Implications of Using the Computer As a Tool in Guidance." In A. G. Watts, E. Stern, and N. Deen (eds.), *Career Guidance Toward the 21st Century.* Cambridge: Careers Research and Advisory Centre, 1993. [www.crac.org.uk]

Open University. *OUTIS Student Survey: Debrief Document.* Milton Keynes, Bucks, U.K.: Open University, 2000.

Phillips, M., Scott, P., and Fage, J. "Toward a Strategy for the Use of New Technology in Student Guidance and Support." *Open Learning,* 1998, 13(2), 52–58.

Quality Assurance Agency for Higher Education. *Subject Review Handbook, September 2000 to December 2001.* Gloucester, U.K.: Quality Assurance Agency, 2000. [www.qaa.ac.uk/SRHbook2/intro.htm]

Sampson, J. P., Kolodinsky, R. W., and Greeno, B. P. "Counselling on the Information Highway: Future Possibilities and Potential Problems." *Journal of Counselling and Development,* 1997, 75, 203–212.

Scott, P., Curson, J., Shipton, G., and McAuley, J. "A Computer-Based Student Welfare Information, Support, and Help System." In P. Carlson and F. Makedon (eds.), *Proceedings of Educational Multimedia and Hypermedia 1996.* Charlottesville, Va.: Association for the Advancement of Computers in Education, 1996.

Scott, P., and Phillips, M. "Developing Web-Based Student Support Systems: Telling Student Stories on the Internet." In M. Eisenstadt and T. Vincent (eds.), *The Knowledge Web: Learning and Collaborating on the Net.* London: Kogan Page, 1998.

Tait, A. "Face-to-Face and at a Distance: The Mediation of Guidance and Counselling Through the New Technologies." *British Journal of Guidance and Counselling,* 1999, 27(1), 113–122.

Vincent, T., and Whalley, P. "The Web: Enabler or Disabler." In M. Eisenstadt and T. Vincent (eds.), *The Knowledge Web: Learning and Collaborating on the Net.* London: Kogan Page, 1998.

Watts, A. G. "Computers in Guidance." In A. G. Watts, B. Law, J. Killeen, J. M. Kidd, and R. Hawthorn (eds.), *Rethinking Careers Education and Guidance: Theory, Policy, and Practice.* London: Routledge, 1996.

MARION PHILLIPS and PATRICK KELLY are assistant directors of student services at The Open University, United Kingdom.

3

Understanding information literacy requires understanding how literacy is changed by electronic technology. Critical literacy is an essential characteristic of information-literate learners.

Extending Information Literacy in Electronic Environments

Sandra Kerka

About 50 percent of American adults are literate at the third, fourth, and fifth levels of literacy measured by the National Adult Literacy Survey (http://nces.ed.gov/naal/naal92/). But how many are information-literate? Does information literacy mean being able to find information in libraries or on the Web? Or does it have broader implications for teaching and learning in the electronic environment of the new millennium? Information literacy has been called a survival skill for the information age (Jackson, 1995), a liberal art (Shapiro and Hughes, 1996), the key competency for the twenty-first century (Bundy, 1998), and the zeitgeist of the times (Candy, 1996). It has been described as "an educational, societal, and democratic issue that should be of fundamental concern to all those who would call themselves educators" (Bundy, 1998); citation taken from Web site). Every day, we must regularly manage more and more information for life and work, using an expanding array of technologies (Marchionini, 1995). Societal expectations of an educated person now include the following abilities: using multiple symbol systems, applying knowledge, thinking strategically, managing information, and learning, thinking, and creating in collaboration with others (Walker, 1999). Such expectations challenge adult educators as never before.

Information literacy is connected to the discourse of lifelong learning and participatory democracy. The American Library Association (ALA) states: "Preparation for independent information retrieval is essential for sustaining lifelong professional and personal growth, and it is basic to almost every aspect of living in a democratic society" (Jackson, 1995, pp. 39–40). The National Institute for Literacy's newly issued standards for adult literacy and lifelong learning note that "in order to carry out daily responsibilities at home, in the community, and in the workplace, adults . . . are required to sift through a vast amount of information" (Stein, 2000, p. 1). The lifelong learning skills outlined under two of the standards—"learn from research" and "use information and communications technology"—echo many of the definitions of information literacy.

These definitions focus on the ability to find, evaluate, use, and communicate information from a variety of sources to solve problems and make decisions (Lenox and Walker, 1993; Spitzer, Eisenberg, and Lowe, 1999; Tyner, 1998). Some of the definitions view information literacy as a tool of empowerment, and ALA's vision seeks to develop "independent seekers of truth" (Jackson, 1995, p. 40). However, much of the focus of current literature and instruction is limited to the "how" of information skills. We need to focus more attention on the "why" and "for what purpose" as the rapidly evolving electronic environment demands that we rethink the notion of literacy: "An irreversible movement from printed to electronic forms of reading and writing points to fundamental changes in the way we communicate and disseminate information, the way we approach the task of reading and writing, and the way we think about helping people become literate" (Reinking, 1995, p. 17)

So I will explore the concept of information literacy as one of a group of literacies needed to thrive in the contemporary environment. I do not focus on the mechanics of information seeking and types of information sources. Instead, I examine how the concept of literacy is changing in the electronic environment in ways that impose an overarching need for critical literacy, and I present issues related to information literacy that adult educators should consider. I use the terms *electronic* and *digital technology* interchangeably, in that digitized means "transformed into electronic bits" (Menzies, 1997, p. 45).

I write as someone who has spent most of her professional life accessing, synthesizing, and helping people to find information and for whom information seeking has become enmeshed in daily life. It has been salutary to reflect on this process and its implications, although the resulting chapter demonstrates some of the limitations of the "ink and dead trees" format of the chapters in this volume (see Howard Rheingold, http://www.rheingold.com/vc/book/). How much better to have been able to present this synthesis hypertextually in order to illustrate the fascinating branches, iterations, and linkages of the information-seeking process that went into the weaving of it!

Digitizing Literacy: Threat or Promise?

In considering whether digital technology changes literacy, we should remember that literacy itself is "above all a technology or set of techniques for communicating, and for decoding and reproducing written or printed materials" (Graff, 1995, p. 10). Literacy technologies themselves have evolved. Just as print did not eliminate oral communication, radio and television did not eliminate books, and the "shift from print to the computer does not mean the end of literacy. What will be lost is not literacy itself, but the literacy of print, for electronic technology offers us a new kind of book and new ways to write and read" (Bolter, 1991, p. 2). So what is different about literacy in a digital environment?

Digital technologies change reading and writing in several fundamental ways (Reinking, 1994). First, electronic texts have different structures such as hypertext, which require new reading strategies. Second, symbolic elements such as animation, graphics, sound, and live-action video are more integrated with prose; more than ever, we must consciously think about the meaning of nonverbal elements. Third, and most important, reader and text can interact in a literal way. The size, shape, and scale of digital text can be controlled by the reader; text can be easily and quickly manipulated, and word, image, and sound are powerfully integrated (Peters and Lankshear, 1996). We are challenged to impose our own conceptual organization on text presented in a nonlinear way, and we must use a range of knowledge to make meaning from these linguistic, symbolic, auditory, and visual aspects of electronic text.

Some see the impact of the digital environment on literacy as an opportunity, and others perceive it as a threat. Tuman (cited in Lanham, 1993) suggests that, without the experience of print literacy, future generations may lack training in linear argument and left-brain conceptualization. However, Lanham argues that electronic text balances rather than supplants left-brain thinking, and Kress (1998) proposes that what we lose in "rationality" we gain in better visual analysis, what he terms *electronic orality*. Tuman states that hypertexts are not texts but systems for storing and retrieving information. He asks: "Is it possible for the ascendancy of hypertext to do anything but push literacy in the direction of information management?" (Lanham, 1993, p. 218). Comparing the rational mind with the "hypermind," Campbell (1998) finds that the hypermind lacks self-knowledge, is prey to sensory stimulation, exhibits poor communication and thinking skills, and lacks metacognitive abilities. Marchionini (1995) counters: "Additional levels of learning and cognitive effort are necessary to use, interpret, and validate information based on electronic digital expressions" (p. 3).

In fact, our assumptions about linear thinking have been shaped by the dimensions (and limitations) of print—the top-down, left-right, beginning-end order of words on a page. However, "hypertexts remind us that acquiring the discipline to organize one's thoughts into a linear, hierarchical argument is a large part of what we call being literate only because the technology of print does not invite other ways to structure an argument, not because that is the natural way we think" (Reinking, 1995, p. 24). Guay (1995) considers hypertext a "biological form of presenting information that models how our mind processes, organizes, and retrieves information as opposed to the artificial linearity of print" (citation taken from Web site).

In what we may call the *typographic world,* literacy was defined by the dominant technology of print. In the *post-typographic world* (Reinking, 1995), electronic technologies are redefining literacy in promising ways, but they also have their dark side. Digital technologies lend an aura of authority to the information found using them. Seduced by the transparency of the interface, ease of access, and aesthetic attractions of the Web, many people willingly suspend disbelief. Comparisons of experts and novices show that "novices often expect that information obtained from a computer will be more exhaustive and more accurate" (Marchionini, 1995, p. 15). In the virtual world, multimedia affects the message: images and graphic design can be manipulated to achieve the developers' aims, and the associative logic of hypertext may illustrate how ideas connect but it can also lead users to false connections and disguise hidden agendas (Labbo, Reinking, and McKenna, 1998).

Although people are becoming technically adept at the mechanics of Internet use, many tend to believe such sources are more current and useful *because* they are online. Because electronic sources are so easy to acquire, print sources are frequently ignored even when they are more appropriate. Cheek and Doskatsch (1998) give the example of a nursing student who became frustrated when using a CD-ROM database to find a definition for *psychology,* failing to recognize that a print dictionary was the faster and more appropriate tool. Not every information need is best served by electronic technology.

The proliferation of new technologies strains our capacity to keep current. We are challenged both by an overload of information and by our frequent failure to retrieve relevant information. Sometimes the syntax and semantics of search tools impede rather than assist us in finding the information we need. The Internet lacks the filtering mechanisms of traditional library resources, and subtle cues that existed in print sources (paper, ink, binding) are no longer available (Fornaciari and Loffredo Roca, 1999). In addition, digital information is both more and less accessible because we must use electronic tools to acquire and use it (Marchionini, 1995).

Media theorists point out that electronic environments magnify the social and cultural biases of information. Semali (1994) presents four postulations about media that he thinks are equally true about curriculum and instruction: (1) worldview, information, and perspectives created by both media and curricula are constructions of reality; (2) audiences negotiate meaning, and different audiences respond to messages presented in media and curricula in different ways; (3) media messages and curricula represent ideology and values, privileging certain sectors of society; and (4) media messages as well as curricula can affect social attitudes and behavior.

Thus, electronic technologies have broader social and cultural consequences. We need both technical skills for using new technologies and cognitive skills for assessing the social context and consequences of the role of technology (Fornaciari and Loffredo Roca, 1999; Luke, 1997). Information literacy should enable individuals both to locate and use information effectively and to think critically about its social origins, structure, and impact (Shapiro and Hughes, 1996). A primary focus for information literacy should be "on developing an awareness of other knowledge domains and belief systems of how knowledge is produced and validated" (Bundy, 1998; citation taken from Web site). In the next section I describe both halves of the equation that makes up an information-literate person: *information skills* and *critical habits of mind.*

From Information Literacy to Critical Literacy

Information literacy involves the development and maintenance of what Marchionini (1995) calls *personal information infrastructures.* These infrastructures reflect the characteristics of expertise: a richly structured information base, recognition of meaningful patterns of information, contextualized knowledge, and fluent retrieval of relevant information (Bransford, Brown, and Cocking, 1999). These infrastructures are developed—and information literacy is acquired—through the process of seeking answers to personally meaningful questions.

The information-seeking process is dependent on an individual's context and culture, and it reflects elements of constructivist behavior: processing information, solving problems, assessing one's learning, and adding new information to existing knowledge structures. The capacities needed for the information-seeking process include understanding information, planning and executing search strategies, and assessing and using information (Marchionini, 1995; Spitzer, Eisenberg, and Lowe, 1999):

- *Understanding:* One understands by becoming aware of the complexities of the information environment and information technologies; articulating an information need; and defining the problem, question, or task.
- *Planning or executing:* One plans or executes by formulating a search strategy; selecting tools and sources and assessing their appropriateness for the task; and retrieving information and evaluating results for accuracy, relevance, and comprehensiveness.
- *Assessing and using information:* One assesses or uses information by engaging with retrieved information (reading, viewing, questioning, reflecting, extracting); manipulating, organizing, and synthesizing information; integrating new information into existing knowledge structures; using it to make decisions, take action, construct meaning; and evaluating the entire process.

This information-seeking process was adequate in a print-dominated world and the skills are still applicable in the twenty-first century. However, new technologies demand additional abilities. One way to define literacy is the ability to decode messages (Lenox and Walker, 1993). Now the messages are coming at us in a variety of written and nonwritten forms, and we need "multiliteracies" to interpret them. These include a number of interrelated literacies (Spitzer, Eisenberg, and Lowe, 1999; Tyner, 1998), including tool literacies and representational literacies.

- *Tool literacies:* These include computer literacy, or understanding how to use hardware and software; network literacy, or awareness and understanding of global networked information resources; and technology literacy, or comprehension of technological innovation and the impact of technology on society.
- *Representational literacies:* These include information literacy; media literacy, or the ability to understand, produce, and negotiate meanings in images, words, and sounds in all types of media; and visual literacy, or the ability to decode, create, and use images in a variety of media.

New terms have been proposed to represent this confluence of literacies. *Cyberliteracy* refers to social practices in which texts are constructed, transmitted, received, modified, and shared through electronically digitized codes (Lankshear and Knobel, 1997). *Electronic* or *e-literacy* refers to reading and writing processes specific to electronic texts, which encompass a range of digitally encoded materials (Kaplan, 1995). *Digital literacy* refers to the ability to recognize, interpret, and evaluate the underlying ideologies in various types of hypertextually linked information (Labbo, Reinking, and McKenna, 1998).

The combined knowledge and skills represented by each of the multiliteracies is necessary for dealing with the digital world, but not sufficient. As electronic technologies present us with the promise of empowerment and the threat of manipulation, *critical literacy* is the overarching concept that links the multiliteracies. Critical literacy involves "reading the world," taking a questioning stance, analyzing both the form and the content of communication. A critically reflective approach is essential to take us beyond a narrow focus on technical skills and "into spaces of inquiry and learning that require engagement with the cultural and social dimensions of electronic technology" (Knobel, 1998; citation taken from Web site).

Critical literacy in electronic environments involves questioning media in the following ways (Knobel, 1998; Peters and Lankshear, 1996; Tyner, 1998):

- Who communicates and why? What type of "text" is it? How is it produced? How do we know what it means? Who receives it? What sense do they make of it? How does it present its subject?
- What version of events is provided? Whose version is it? From whose perspective is it presented? What versions are excluded? Whose interests

are served by it? By what means does the text construct reality? How does the text position the reader?

- What kind of readers would find this text unproblematic? What would they believe, value, espouse? What account of reality is provided and how does the text construct this reality through grammar and syntax? Who is in the text and who is written out of it and why?
- Why and how have these technologies become available? Who shapes their forms and effects? For what purposes?

At a minimum, critical habits of thought prevent users of electronic technologies from becoming victims of fraud and misinformation, from uncritically accepting and using electronic sources. However, the transition from print to electronic text opens the opportunity for "expanded and enhanced practices of critical literacy" (Peters and Lankshear, 1996, p. 53). This critical metaliteracy can help us understand the political and material consequences of technological change, how it will change our lives, and who will benefit from or be disadvantaged by it (Luke, 1997). Armed with a critical mindset, individuals can reflect on and question assumptions about technology as a panacea, about whether information should be considered a commodity or a public good, about the loss of privacy and the potential for surveillance, about the corporatizing of the Internet and whether global networking can realize its democratizing potential or serve to strengthen the cultural hegemony of certain sectors of society. This "extended notion of information literacy is essential to the future of democracy, if citizens are to be part of a meaningful existence rather than a routine of production and consumption" (Shapiro and Hughes, 1996 [citation taken from Web site]).

Issues and Trends

This concluding section outlines some of the issues and trends related to information literacy as it affects adult educators' use of technology. Three areas are addressed: *redefining literacy; access, equity, and power;* and *teaching and learning with technologies*.

Redefining Literacy. Print-based literacy may not disappear soon, for a number of reasons. For the moment, a fair amount of what we see on the Web is still being treated like printed texts (Peters and Lankshear, 1996). Portability, bandwidth, and cost still pose barriers. Therefore, print-based technologies continue to have a place in teaching (Burge, 1999; O'Rourke, this volume), and learners need to apply information literacy skills to both print and electronic resources.

At the same time, there are signs that digital environments are reshaping the way we think about literacy. Yet Campbell (1998) fears that these technologies force lateral thinking, not deep understanding, that they overstimulate the brain's visual, rather than verbal, acuity. Can it not be said that print culture has overstimulated verbal acuity for centuries? As electronic environments demand both linear cognitive skills *and* hypertext reading skills, we have the opportunity to balance and develop both visual and verbal acuity, as well as convergent and divergent thinking.

Access, Equity, and Power. Two views of the emerging digital world can be discerned. Some people welcome the coming of the so-called global village, formed by the democratization of communication and information. The bypassing of traditional sources of authority and power changes the politics of publication and dissemination, enabling many groups, cultures, and subcultures to find a voice (Luke, 1997; Peters and Lankshear, 1996). Other people argue that access to information is far from universal and is being limited by the increasing control of technologies by conglomerates that view information as a commodity (Menzies, 1997). The number of resources available only electronically and for a fee is increasing, and a "digital divide" based on class, gender, race, and economics is growing. Of what use is information literacy if individuals cannot afford access?

Tyner (1998) worries that focusing simply on access obscures issues that may actually help redress social inequities—critical thinking, knowledge creation, and lifelong learning opportunities. Menzies (1997) recasts the issue of access in terms of two contrasting models of communication: an ecological model focused on social relationships and a transmission model in which information is a commodity. In the transmission model, access is defined as access to technology; in the ecological model, access to meaningful participation is paramount. Menzies stresses that educators do not have to choose one or the other, but they should consider the two models and the values they reflect when teaching with and about electronic technologies. Is the purpose of education forming human beings or "in-forming" consumers (de Castell, 1998)?

We must also consider that information is a privileged term in Western societies (Cheek and Doskatsch, 1998) but may have different meanings in other cultures. Culture and learning style affect our approach to information seeking. Bruce and Hogan (1998) urge us to think critically about what we accept as normal in our technological tools. Computer interfaces largely reflect Western culture in the metaphor of a desktop, the icons used, and the English-language defaults, rendering other cultures invisible. We may blame the user for inability to use a tool (information *illiteracy*) when it may be design choices reflecting the dominant culture that put the user at a disadvantage.

Teaching and Learning in Electronic Environments. The educational promise of electronic technologies will not be realized if digital texts are used merely to transmit information and deliver instruction (Peters and Lankshear, 1996). The "primary goal of educational uses of technology is to foster the habits of mind, the skills, and the conceptual insights required for participation" in the digital world (Labbo, Reinking, and McKenna, 1998, p. 281).

Constructivist teaching and learning have much in common with the information-seeking process, so they should support each other. To learn constructively involves active processing of new information, structured experiential activity, critical analysis, acceptance of ambiguity, and metacognition (Wilson and Lowry, this volume). Constructivism is based on the recognition that knowledge is socially constructed. The literacies identified in this article are a set of technologies and social practices acquired through participation in social relationships. Adult education settings should be dynamic social environments in which learners collaborate in assembling, analyzing, and synthesizing information gathered from electronic and non-electronic sources.

The new electronic orality identified by Kress (1998) and bemoaned by Tuman may give rise to "a new kind of interactive discourse akin to conversation" (Tuman, cited in Kaplan, 1995). Guay (1995) contends that the "Web returns us to a more oral notion, that of ongoing conversation, one that spans the globe" [citation taken from Web site]. One way to view teaching and learning is as an extended conversation among co-learners, and electronic environments thus extend the opportunities for social learning.

Threat and Promise. The electronic environment enormously increases access to information (for many), which enormously magnifies a problem that has existed as long as there has been information: How good is it? Can I trust it? Is that all there is? I know how to find it using these techniques, but what happens when the technology changes?

There is great promise in electronic access to information and the resulting democratization of publication and dissemination. At the same time, the potential threats make a framework of critical literacy essential. And in this fluid environment, we should think of information literacy and the related multiliteracies as not an end state but a developmental process (Leu, 1997). In this context, information literacy may be viewed as a way of learning that can be applied to all types of technologies, electronic or not.

Web Sites Related to Information Literacy

This list of resources may prove of interest to readers seeking to learn more about information literacy.

- *Directory of Online Resources for Information Literacy,* edited by Drew Smith, University of South Florida [http://nosferatu.cas.usf.edu/lis/il/]. This is a collection of links in the following categories: assessment, bibliographies and Webographies, conferences, definitions, electronic mailing lists, the information literacy process, organizations and projects, papers and presentations, programs in higher education, programs in K–12 education, tutorials.

- *Using Educational Technology to Teach Information Literacy.* Winter term workshop for faculty, Oberlin College, January 7–16, 1998 [http://www.oberlin.edu/~OCTET/workshops/InfoLit/Default.html]. This workshop covered the following topics: the challenge of "infoglut" and the need for information literacy in the digital age, creating online syllabi and other Web-based course materials, electronic access to information resources, options for supplementing classroom interaction, strategies for teaching information literacy.
- *Doing Research from a Distance,* Council of Atlantic University Libraries [http://www.mun.ca/library/ref/li/caul/research.html]. This was written especially for students who are taking courses through distance education.
- *Info Search: A Step-by-Step Guide to Finding Information for a Research Assignment,* University of New Brunswick Libraries [http://www.lib.unb.ca/library/instruction/InfoSearch.html]. Topics include defining your topic, understanding types of publications, discovering electronic information sources, searching databases, retrieving and evaluating your results, writing your paper and bibliography.
- *The Cyberspace, Hypertext, and Critical Theory Web: An Introduction,* by George P. Landow, Brown University [http://landow.stg.brown.edu/cpace/cspaceov.html]. This is a searchable collection of resources on cyberspace, hypertext, critical theory, information technology, and other topics.

References

Bolter, J. D. *Writing Space: The Computer, Hypertext, and the History of Writing.* Hillsdale, N.J.: Erlbaum, 1991.

Bransford, J. D., Brown, A. L., and Cocking, R. R. (eds.). *How People Learn: Brain, Mind, Experience, and School.* Washington, D.C.: National Academy Press, 1999.

Bruce, B. C., and Hogan, M. P. "The Disappearance of Technology: Toward an Ecological Model of Literacy." In D. Reinking, M. C. McKenna, L. D. Labbo, and R. D. Kieffer (eds.), *Handbook of Literacy and Technology: Transformations in a Post-Typographic World* (pp. 269–281). Hillsdale, N.J.: Erlbaum, 1998.

Bundy, A. L. "Information Literacy: The Key Competency for the 21st Century." Paper presented at the International Association of Technological University Libraries Conference, Pretoria, South Africa, June 1998. [http://educate.lib.chalmers.se/iatul/proceedcontents/pretpap/bundy.html]

Burge, E. J. "Using Learning Technologies: Ideas for Keeping One's Balance." *Educational Technology,* 1999, 39(6), 45–49.

Campbell, R. J. "HyperMinds for HyperTimes: The Demise of Rational, Logical Thought?" *Educational Technology,* 1998, 38(1), 24–31. (EJ 559 832)

Candy, P. "Major Themes and Future Directions." In D. Booker (ed.), *Learning for Life: Information Literacy and the Autonomous Learner.* Adelaide: University of South Australia, 1996.

Cheek, J., and Doskatsch, I. "Information Literacy: A Resource for Nurses as Lifelong Learners." *Nurse Education Today,* 1998, 18(3), 243–250. (EJ 567 033)

de Castell, S. "From Data and Information to Learning and Understanding." *Education Canada,* 1998, 38(1), 9–19. [http://www.educ.sfu.ca/gentech/libweb.htm]

Fornaciari, C. J., and Loffredo Roca, M. F. "The Age of Clutter: Conducting Effective

Research Using the Internet." *Journal of Management Education*, 1999, 23(6), 732–742.

Graff, H. J. *The Labyrinths of Literacy*. Pittsburgh, Penn.: University of Pittsburgh Press, 1995.

Guay, T. "Web Publishing Paradigms." [http://hoshi.cic.sfu.ca/~guay/Paradigm/]. April 1995.

Jackson, S. "Information Literacy and Public Libraries: A Community-Based Approach." In *Information for a New Age: Redefining the Librarian* (pp. 35–45). Englewood, Colo.: Libraries Unlimited, 1995.

Kaplan, N. "E-literacies: Politexts, Hypertexts, and Other Cultural Formations in the Late Age of Print." *Computer-Mediated Communication*, 1995, 2(3). [http://metalab. unc.edu/cmc/mag/1995/mar/kaplan.html]

Knobel, M. "Critical Literacy and New Technologies." Paper prepared for Research in the Teaching of English, June 1998. [http://www.schools.ash.org.au/litweb/ michele.html]

Kress, G. "Visual and Verbal Modes of Representation in Electronically Mediated Communication." In I. Snyder (ed.), *Page to Screen: Taking Literacy into the Electronic Era* (pp. 53–79). New York: Routledge, 1998.

Labbo, L. D., Reinking, D., and McKenna, M. C. "Technology and Literacy Education in the Next Century." *Peabody Journal of Education*, 1998, 73(3–4), 273–289. (EJ 588 813)

Lanham, R. A. *The Electronic Word*. Chicago: University of Chicago Press, 1993.

Lankshear, C., and Knobel, M. "Critical Literacy and Active Citizenship." In S. Muspratt, A. Luke, and P. Freebody (eds.), *Constructing Critical Literacies: Teaching and Learning Textual Practice* (pp. 95–124). Cresskill, N.J.: Hampton Press, 1997.

Lenox, M. F., and Walker, M. L. "Information Literacy in the Educational Process." *Educational Forum*, 1993, 57(2), 312–324. (EJ 465 008)

Leu, D. J., Jr. "Caity's Question: Literacy as Deixis on the Internet." *Reading Teacher*, 1997, 51(1), 62–67.

Luke, C. *Technological Literacy*. Research into Practice Series, no. 4. Melbourne, Australia: National Languages and Literacy Institute, 1997. (ED 430 087)

Marchionini, G. *Information Seeking in Electronic Environments*. New York: Cambridge University Press, 1995.

Menzies, H. "The Digital New Economy and the Virtual Educator." *Canadian Journal of University Continuing Education*, 1997, 23(2), 43–59.

Peters, M., and Lankshear, C. "Digital Literacy and Digital Texts." *Educational Theory*, 1996, 46(1), 51–70.

Reinking, D. *Electronic Literacy*. Perspectives in Reading Research, no. 4. Athens: University of Georgia, and College Park: University of Maryland, National Reading Research Center, 1994. (ED 371 324)

Reinking, D. "Reading and Writing with Computers: Literacy Research in a Post-Typographic World." In K. A. Hinchman, D. J. Leu, and C. K. Kinzer (eds.), *Perspectives on Literacy Research and Practice* (pp. 17–33). Chicago: National Reading Conference, 1995.

Semali, L. M. "Teaching Critical Literacy across the Curriculum in Multimedia America." Paper presented at the 44th Annual Meeting of the National Reading Conference, San Diego, Calif., November 30–December 3, 1994. (ED 380 762)

Shapiro, J. J., and Hughes, S. K. "Information Literacy as a Liberal Art." *Educom Review*, 1996, 31(2). [http://www.educause.edu/pub/er/review/reviewarticles/31231.html]

Spitzer, K. L., Eisenberg, M. B., and Lowe, C. A. *Information Literacy: Essential Skills for the Information Age*. Syracuse, N.Y.: ERIC Clearinghouse on Information and Technology, Syracuse University, 1999. (ED 427 780)

Stein, S. *Equipped for the Future Content Standards. What Adults Need to Know and Be Able to Do in the 21st Century*. Washington, D.C.: National Institute for Literacy, 2000.

Tyner, K. *Literacy in a Digital World: Teaching and Learning in the Age of Information.* Hillsdale, N.J.: Erlbaum, 1998.

Walker, D. "Technology and Literacy: Raising the Bar." *Educational Leadership,* 1999, 57(2), 18–21.

SANDRA KERKA is associate director of the ERIC Clearinghouse on Adult, Career, and Vocational Education, the Ohio State University, and editor–Web master of OhioDance in Columbus.

4

Although unintended effects cannot be anticipated,
practitioners can use various frameworks to recognize
and manage them.

Unintended Effects in Using Learning Technologies

Allan Herrmann, Robert Fox, Anna Boyd

"[New] technology has its imperatives and its preferences. It makes its demands. To introduce the computer into a social environment does not result in the same environment plus computers, just as the introduction of an exotic animal into a natural environment does not result in the same environment plus the animal. All things change to accommodate the exotic" (Arnold, 1999, p. 90).

Unexpected effects resulting from the introduction of technologies are not new. As Postman explains (1992), the introduction of the stirrup was intended merely to help the rider stay on the horse, but no one could foresee its leading to the presence of a new societal group—the knight class—which in turn created further unintended effects. The invention and use of the automobile showed similar cascading, visible and invisible unintended effects. More recently, MacIntosh (1992) reported on the installation of a new telephone system in a remote area of Western Australia: "Virtually every station eagerly paid up. The advantages of 24-hour availability, clear communication, and privacy made the telephone the highest priority for capital expenditure" (p. 1). One effect of the telephone installations, which was not immediately obvious, was the loss of community: no longer could neighbors spend long periods talking on two-way radio at virtually no cost. The new technology was supposed to support and develop the region rather than to reduce its sense of community.

Our experience has taught us that as soon as any technology is introduced into the teaching and learning contexts, it affects, either intentionally or unintentionally, what happens: sometimes for better, sometimes for worse. Therefore, we identify here the importance of unintended effects, outline different ways to understand unintended effects, and give examples of unintended effects. We end with some implications for smart practice.

What Are Unintended Effects?

We see them as those effects of the use of learning technologies that are unforeseen by the individual or group using them. That is to say, unintended effects are not misguided applications, consequences of the rate of adoption, poor equipment design, or the known effects of the inherent biases of each medium. For this chapter we see the terms *unintended effects, unintended consequences,* and *second order consequences* (Locatis and Gooler, 1975) as having similar meanings.

The Importance of Unintended Effects

Cost implications, prior peer experience, and the need to manage negative effects are relevant here. During any course design process, responsible fiscal management demands that we analyze (as far as possible) the short- and long-term consequences of any learning technology. This analysis provides benefits for learners in that it helps the design of an efficient and effective learning experience; for teachers and instructors in that they can minimize unproductive time spent fixing errors later; for planners in that they may use past successes for future trials; and for managers in that they may expedite the implementation of programs and save time and money.

We can learn from the experience of others and deliberately think about unexpected effects, even though, by definition, we cannot predict all of them. Being reflective practitioners should help us to think about possible consequences for learners as well as for our own work. Adult learners do not deserve to be unwitting and unwilling techno-guinea pigs. They already carry the burdens of other life roles, so they look for time and energy efficiency.

Different Ways to Understand Unintended Effects

As is true of all efforts to categorize the real world, there is always subjectivity in judgment and much overlapping of categories. Roger Baldwin (1998), in writing about the selective impact of technology on academic life, highlights the variable rates and methods of adoption of technology by organizations and individuals. If the uptake of learning technologies is not always to plan, then the effects of that adoption cannot be planned.

A wise adult educator may think of unintended effects in various ways: (1) Tenner's (1996) revenge theory in which he identifies five possible effects of the introduction of technology—rearranging, repeating, recomplicating, regenerating, and recongesting; (2) privileging, where particular technologies demand or provide certain treatments and exclude others (see Green, Gough, and Blackmore, 1996; Bigum, 1998; and Salomon, 1997, for variations on this theme); (3) changing of power relationships (for example Postman, 1992; see the stirrup example earlier); or (4) adding to or adapting an environment (for example, Evans and Nation, 2000).

Alternatively, a more simplified framework uses three categories: physical, psychosocial, and pedagogical. The physical category encompasses the backache, repetitive strain injury (RSI), and eyestrain, which learners and teachers may suffer as a consequence of poor ergonomics. It also includes the lower efficiency in reading online; for example, reduced readability (Schriver, 1997) and the physical access to the requisite technologies. Adults with physical disabilities are of particular interest. The psychosocial category refers to those unintended effects that affect relationships and interpersonal communications; for example, the loss of face-to-face contact in audioconferencing and most forms of computer conferencing today may have the unintended effect of inhibiting participation or slowing down group development processes. Equally, the economic and social status of users interacting with learning technologies can produce equity-related unintended effects. The pedagogical category may include learners becoming conceptually lost in cyberspace, the learning technology subtly (or not so subtly) redefining the course content and teaching style, the hard-won extra time needed for keeping up to date with new versions of each technology, and the "liberation" of vast amounts of information that is not necessarily essential for the learner's immediate needs.

In each of these groups the unintended effects can be perceived to be positive or negative depending on factors such as time, place, and response to them. For example, in moving to audioconferencing or a Web environment, the expected visual and other paralinguistic cues (Burge, 1999) and clues on which we base much of our reaction to others are lost. What is often reported by staff the first time they teach online is that the new environment seems to allow learners to view and express themselves in different ways, particularly when face-to-face courses move to the Web. Learners who might contribute very little to classroom discussion respond positively to the new environment. Regardless of the actual reason—for example, safe pseudoanonymity—the fact is that these learners enjoy the time available to formulate a response or contribution. The somewhat pejorative term *lurker* signifies noncontributors in online activity, but the use of such a negative label may, in fact, have the unintended effect of forcing some adult learners further into the cybershadows. For other adults, the unintended effect of going online to learn is to see themselves as more competent in self-expression than in face-to-face or voice-to-voice modes—certainly a positive unintended effect.

Examples of Unintended Effects

We group our examples by impact on learner, teacher, and organization.

Learner Examples. Here we see three unintended effects: "playtime," access difficulties, and increased contributive opportunities. Our recent surveys of learners studying online indicate that some appear to spend more time "studying" than they did in traditional courses. We have no reason to believe that our learners are becoming less efficient, so we believe that there is a novelty effect operating where learners seem to enjoy Web browsing and spend additional time surfing—almost playing. Although their teachers intended that learners feel comfortable online and develop the necessary skills, most did not see surfing in itself as an intended outcome. To minimize this technology-induced "opportunity," teachers designed better task instructions and site descriptions and gave time parameters for particular tasks. Learners, particularly those participating from home, may not have access to the range of technology that we might expect. Audioconference classes may rely only on access to the easy-to-use telephone, but in many families there is competition for the telephone, particularly in the evenings. Similarly, competing needs for online access from home may produce conflict and call for a family to use or even develop its own negotiation skills to ensure equitable access and quiet surrounding conditions. As more courses require telecommunications access, the usage levels at home increase. We have anecdotes about mothers who have to "fight" their children and spouse or partner for appropriate access conditions. Conflict can arise also when learners rely on access to learning technologies owned by their employer. Not all employers subscribe to the notion that self-motivated employees should be given free or at least easy access to online services at work.

A colleague taught a course with a field placement component that required students to spend time working in offices, some remote from campus. She used audioconferencing to maintain contact and develop group interaction. She continues:

> At lunchtime every Tuesday fifteen of us would get together and discuss the week. I have had a fair degree of success using audioconferencing and one positive thing using this technology was that with the use of the telephone being a significant part of their work experience, we were able to use these sessions for skills development too. However, some problems that I hadn't anticipated did arise . . . the cost for interstate learners, the time differences across the different states, some learners monopolizing the conversation, some learners feeling very uncomfortable with not being able to see the rest of us and [being] unable to contribute, and one woman having a hearing difficulty and so couldn't keep up with the telephone sessions. Reflecting on these issues, I looked for alternative ways of responding to them. I decided to develop an online learning environment that included a discussion group and

a bulletin board to post up-to-date administrative information about assignments and exams. To avoid the issue of time differences, I decided to use an asynchronous discussion group. It meant that everyone could post when it was convenient so that there would be no conflict between work and class meetings. A bonus was that the woman with the hearing difficulty was able to participate fully. The question of online anonymity had worried me, but in fact the learners assumed pseudonyms and were happy to post all sorts of issues that they had concerns about. I would put my suggestions in, but the exciting unanticipated thing, was that the learners were happy to help each other.

Teacher Examples. How teachers adopt learning technologies is complex (Fox and Herrmann, 2000) and not the focus here. We outline four unintended results: reduced quality of output, unexpected self-awareness, displacement of teaching goals, and counterintuitive behavior.

The use of video for conferencing, tape, or broadcast is usually an attempt to develop quality learning materials. But sometimes quality efforts are extended in very unexpected ways; here is one example. Watching themselves on a videotape or during a videoconference, teachers suddenly see themselves as their learners see them: every idiosyncratic physical feature and behavior is recorded remorselessly. Some teachers retreat, vowing never to do it again, but others reach for professional development.

Alternatively, teachers can deliberately design their use of learning technologies to improve the learners' experience, but in the end they may reduce their own efficiency through added stress. The following (edited) story is not unique.

Not long ago, I got a small grant to help me redevelop my study unit for my distance learners. I decided to develop the unit online. At this point, I saw I had two clear options. I could spend a fair part of the funds on employing a Web-coder to help me get my materials online or I could get myself some time release, learn a bit more about the Web courseware, and write everything myself. I decided this was a good opportunity to learn how to do it all myself. I spent many hours just playing around, finding out new things to do, learning new tricks, and finding new boundaries of what was possible and what was not. At the same time, I had to think how best I could use this technology to get my materials across to my learners. Halfway through the semester, I could see I was running out of time and that I had to speed up or I'd never finish the course materials by the start of semester the unit was on offer. One result of speeding up was I no longer had time to think how best I could use the technology. I had only the time to put the materials I had developed in print onto the Web. I ended up stressed out. I can't say I was thrilled with the results, nor were my learners. To a great extent, I ended up with my print-based course online, with some multiple-choice questions and answers added that bore some but limited relevance to the course. Looking back, it's easy to see I had not worked well or probably done the right thing by deciding to develop the Web site entirely on my own.

In his journal, this teacher noted the unintended effects of the costly use of time, especially because his time cost more to the institution than did a programmer's or Web designer's time, yet his digital skills were less. He also commented on his inappropriate use of the technology. From an organizational perspective this story reflects badly: it shows the unintended effect of the development of a cottage industry mindset and the loss of institutional quality control; that is, the learning design and materials production were not organized into and reviewed through a multiskilled team-based model, as happens in well-established flexible learning institutions.

We also have experience of some teachers creating their own unintended effects because of well-meant but naïve behavior. Here is an example.

I have had many comments from off-campus students indicating that they felt that they were disadvantaged by not having access to lectures and tutorials. I tried to decrease this feeling of them missing out by sending the off-campus students copies of my PowerPoint slides from my lectures. I felt quite virtuous as I sent off the packages to be delivered to my students. The phone started ringing within two days: "How does Power Point slide 3 relate to page 17 in the textbook?" "On PowerPoint slide 7 you list four key attributes, where five were discussed in the guide. Which one was wrong?" they wanted to know. By trying to do the students a favor by sending them the PowerPoint slides, I hadn't considered the commentary that accompanies the slides within a lecture was missing from the off-campus group. I couldn't add the anecdote that explains the complex example in slide 9. By trying to help bridge the gap between on-campus and off-campus students I had actually disenfranchised the off-campus group even more.

Videoconferencing offers real-time and visual interaction, but some counterintuitive behavior is needed to answer such beginners' questions as this: "Where do you look when speaking? Do you look at the camera lens to engage and include the students at other sites (thus ignoring those sitting next to you) or do you look at those around you and hope that the somewhat voyeuristic experiences of the other students (looking in from the psychological outside) will benefit them?" Particularly with low bandwidth or compressed video signals, many participants have problems with the response latency in discussions—that is when verbal and visual cues are not fully synchronized.

Organizational Examples. The following example from our practice highlights the unintended effects of trying to introduce new learning technologies into an organization based on funding individual "early adopters" (Moore, 1995). Senior staff made a strategic decision to promote the use of learning technologies for the improvement of teaching and learning. Central seed funds were set up to encourage technoenthusiasts to develop projects using learning technologies in the hope that they would produce examples of good practice for others to adopt and then adapt to their own teaching. This bottom-up approach brought advantages: the expertise of enthusiasts was rewarded, their hard work often resulted in improvements in their own teaching, their less successful projects gave peers and participants useful lessons, and the competitive funding strategy did not force the participation of less technologically enthusiastic staff. But such competitive funding also generated unintended effects: the projects tended to be small and were developed in isolation, rather than collaboratively. Experienced and talented writers of applications, rather than experienced and talented users of learning technologies, were rewarded with funding. Other staff, including the "later majority" adopters, were not drawn in and continued to be skeptical.

Any organization has to consider the unintended industrial effects of the introduction of learning technologies and the structural changes in the teaching and learning process that the effects stimulate in the organization. Unless managed appropriately, the introduction of learning technologies will blur the functional distinctions between teacher, designer, materials developer, tutor, and administrator; indeed, it can redefine the when and where of the teaching and learning process. When computer-savvy technophiles take pedagogical control of new learning technologies, or assume unwarranted teaching competence, one unintended effect is resistance by more experienced teachers who will look to their skillful peers for guidance or wait until the technology has matured. If some of the unintended negative effects, as argued by David Noble (1998), are to be taken seriously, managers, planners, and adult educators need to be alerted to potential unintended consequences. For many organizations, positive unintended effects of introducing new learning technologies relate to the ability of the organization to clarify the functions of various learning materials and processes and subject them to more rigorous evaluation procedures. The politics of how the organization implements and manages quality control when there are many discrete cottage industries (in teachers' offices) remains, but we believe that the pressure for more reliable measures will increase.

Library services are not immune from the unintended effects of their new learning technologies. Efficiencies allegedly gained by replacing human information-searching with electronic databases or saving shelving space with computer terminals can be overshadowed by the loss of affective help that real librarians give struggling learners (Burge and Snow, 2000) or the loss of less visible functions, such as organizational and professional memory.

In many organizations it is thought that using the new learning technologies will eventually save them money. Yet there is growing evidence that online teaching and learning at present only transfer the costs—from organization to learner, for example. Although that is a short-term gain, it may be a longer-term loss if learners then decide to transfer themselves to a less costly institution. One unintended effect for organizations of the introduction of new learning technologies is the additive effect (as opposed to the replacement effect). The addition of audiotapes, video-tapes, and audio- or videoconferencing and the development of online learning environments has not replaced print, but added to it. For the learner the amount of learning material may become burdensome instead of helpful, for the teacher the materials development and course mainte-nance workload may increase, and for the organization the version control problems, production, and delivery costs may increase. An exam-ple may help to illustrate this effect. In 1982, an institution known to us produced, on average, approximately three thousand study material pages per full-time-equivalent learner. By 1999 the number of print impressions per full-time-equivalent learner had risen to well over four thousand, in spite of the addition of other learning resources.

Implications

Unintended effects cannot always be isolated and categorized into neat and discrete groups. However, we focus on three general subjects to help us think about managing unintended effects.

The first focus is *design and development.* Simple operation is better than complex. It is important to identify the reasons for using the learning technology and the benefits and problems it brings to any context; reduce the temptations to be swept along by novelty. How might the proposed technologies privilege certain teaching models or learning activities or strategies or users? Trial before use is best—if possible in the actual envi-ronment—and then asking a colleague to assist and assess: he or she may see effects to which the educator is blind. Team-based approaches to learn-ing materials design, particularly when dealing with sophisticated tech-nologies, usually reduce the possibility of unintended effects. It is important to allow adult learners and the support staff enough time for "bedding down" the learning technology—that is, rendering it reliable and very easy to use.

The second focus is the *user.* It is important to be honest with but not scare learners, teachers, or colleagues about the possibilities of unintended effects on their preferred learning styles and the necessary learning strate-gies (refer to the Olgren chapter in this volume). No untested assumptions should be made about which learning technologies adults may prefer; for example, a technology that keeps a learner housebound may be detrimen-tal to that learner's effectiveness. Adults, particularly novices, tend to think that unexpected occurrences are unique to them and caused by their mis-use of the technology; they can be reassured that some problems are grounded in poor design (Norman, 1993). Some unintended effects may be the result of circumstances well outside the educator's immediate control—for example, lack of consistent access to a home computer. Educators should accept this and work with the individuals to resolve their challenges. When an unintended effect is positive, the learner should be encouraged to share it with peers.

The third focus is *feedback*. No adult educator is omniscient. It is essential to seek feedback constantly, both formally and informally, on intended and unintended effects of any course process. Then, it is important to do something about what is found out—acknowledge the learners' help and take remedial action. Adults like to feel ownership in any learning activity.

In this chapter we have offered ideas that now may appear to be too obvious for the chapter they consume. But therein lies the point: hindsight is easier to manage than foresight. Unintended effects will appear after we relax our attention, and a negative effect may not easily indicate its positive potential. To be forewarned is the best preparation.

References

Arnold, M. "The Virtual University." *ARENA*, 1999, *13*, 85–100.

Baldwin, R. G. "Technology's Impact on Faculty Life and Work." In K. H. Gillespie (ed.), *The Impact of Technology on Faculty Development, Life, and Work.* New Directions for Teaching and Learning, no. 76. San Francisco: Jossey-Bass, 1998.

Bigum, C. "Boundaries, Barriers and Borders: Teaching Science in a Wired World." *Australian Science Teachers Journal*, 1998, *44*(1), 13–24.

Burge, E. "Using Learning Technologies: Ideas for Keeping One's Balance." *Educational Technology*, 1999, *39*(6), 45–49.

Burge, E., and Snow, J. "Candles, Corks, and Contracts: Essential Relationships Between Learners and Librarians." *New Review of Libraries and Lifelong Learning*, 2000, *1*(1), 19–34.

Evans, T., and Nation, D. "Understanding Changes to University Teaching." In T. Evans and D. Nation (eds.), *Changing University Teaching: Reflections on Creating Educational Technologies.* London: Kogan Page, 2000.

Fox, R., and Herrmann, A. "Changing Media, Changing Times: Coping with New Technology Adoption." In T. Evans and D. Nation (eds.), *Changing University Teaching: Reflections on Creating Educational Technologies.* London: Kogan Page, 2000.

Green, B., Gough, N., and Blackmore, J. (eds.). *Australian Educational Researcher.* Geelong, Victoria: Australian Association for Research in Education, 1996.

Locatis, C., and Gooler, D. "Evaluating Second-Order Consequences: Technology Assessment and Education." *Review of Educational Research*, 1975, *45*(2), 327–353.

MacIntosh, J. *Improving Local Networking for Outback Women* [report]. Western Australia State Government, Western Australian Women's Trust, 1992.

Moore, G. A. *Crossing the Chasm: Marketing and Selling High-Tech Products to Mainstream Customers.* New York: HarperCollins, 1995.

Noble, D. "Digital Diploma Mills: The Automation of Higher Education." *Monthly Review*, 1998, *49*(9) 38–52. [See also http://communication.ucsd.edu/dl/index.html.]

Norman, D. A. *Things That Make Us Smart: Defending Human Attributes in the Age of the Machine.* Reading, Mass.: Addison-Wesley, 1993.

Postman, N. *Technopoly: The Surrender of Culture to Technology.* New York: Knopf, 1992.

Salomon, G. "Of Mind and Media: How Culture's Symbolic Forms Affect Learning and Teaching." *Phi Delta Kappan*, 1997, *78*(5), 375–380.

Schriver, K. *Dynamics in Document Design.* New York: Wiley, 1997.

Tenner, E. *Why Things Bite Back: Technology and the Revenge of Unintended Consequences.* New York: Knopf, 1996.

ALLAN HERRMANN is a senior lecturer in open, distance, and flexible learning at the Centre for Educational Advancement, Curtin University of Technology, Australia.

ROBERT FOX is a senior lecturer at the Centre for Educational Advancement, Curtin University of Technology, Australia.

ANNA BOYD is a lecturer at the Centre for Educational Advancement, Curtin University of Technology, Australia.

5

*Print provides a model for many other learning technolo-
gies. Good design and thoughtful applications can make
the best use of its main assets—durability, flexibility, and
accessibility.*

Print

Jennifer O'Rourke

Print is so much a part of our learning lives that we take it for granted. As
McLuhan observed, a pervasive medium becomes invisible: we are rarely
aware of the air that surrounds us (McLuhan, 1964). Print is still central to
many types of learning and is also a significant part of many of the electronic media that claim to displace it.

Here, we consider print as a learning technology, distinct from its many
other roles (for example, as a news or entertainment medium). We focus on
how print works as a learning medium and how to make the best use of these
features. Print refers to paper-based learning materials, and includes words,
images, graphics, and photographs presented in a visual format and captured
on a permanent one-dimensional surface. Print is also the original medium
of convergence: it can be used for individual and group learning, with or
without the presence of a teacher or mentor, in a variety of formal and informal learning contexts. This chapter focuses on situations in which the print
medium carries a significant proportion of the instructional dynamic, in open
and distance learning, and in resource-based learning in the classroom or in
informal settings, such as libraries or local learning centers.

The practical attributes of print that make it ideal as a learning technology include its durability, portability, and accessibility. It does not require additional tools or equipment to use and is available to almost everyone: even
people who cannot read can learn from print images and charts. Print can be
used to support a wide range of learning tasks and learning styles, and it
enables the learner to respond in kind. In other words, learners themselves can
create print, which empowers them, in Freirian terms, to act as "subjects" in
the learning process, rather than as passive recipients of content (Friere, 1983).

But these same attributes can present problems. The durability of print
can make it more costly and time consuming to alter and update than the

more ephemeral media. The authority of print, based on its physical durability and our everyday uses of it as a reliable source of information, can
intimidate the learner. Its universality means that print is regarded as very
ordinary.

Examining the Different Uses of Print as a Learning Technology

Print as a learning technology can be described in terms of its use: to learn
from, to learn with, and to learn beside.

We *learn from* print, using print resources and reference materials that
present information and ideas that stimulate learning, enabling users to
build up their knowledge base and to develop understanding. Learners can
consult the print resources and can decide what to "take in" or not, but they
cannot directly change the resources themselves.

We *learn with* print materials that serve as a companion for learning,
such as study guides, how-to books, or user manuals. They serve as a guide,
providing direction and opportunities to interact with the materials. Learners engage with the print material in a more direct way, and they can use it
to build their own understanding and comprehension.

We *learn beside* print materials that serve as an extension or expression
of ourselves as learners: we use learning journals, working notes, and assignments to record ideas and responses to the resources and the process of learning itself. Print is a means of "outing" ideas, placing ideas outside ourselves
where they can be considered and examined by ourselves and by others.

Learning from Print

Print is the mainstay medium for presenting information and ideas. It allows
users to read, review, and revisit the material, and to incorporate it into their
own sphere of knowledge. Bates (1995, p. 120) quotes Iser's description of
the process: "(Reading) sets in motion a whole chain of activities that
depend both on the text and on the exercise of certain basic human facul-
ties. Effects and responses are properties neither of the text nor of the
reader; the text represents a potential effect that is realized in the reading
process" (Iser, 1978).

The types of content that can be presented in print cover a broad spec-
trum; from abstract, theoretical concepts to the detailed description of a
physical process. The principles guiding best use of print as a presentation
medium depend very much on the content and the learners. What works
for conveying the philosophy of religion to university students is unlikely
to be effective for communicating the principles of hydraulics to secondary
school technical students.

Although open and distance learning is not by any means the only use
of print as a learning technology, the demands of ODL serve as a useful real-

ity check when considering the instructional design of print materials. Good design enables learners to work independently, interactively, and successfully with the materials. If materials can be structured so that distance learners can use them effectively to achieve their learning goals, without direct face-to-face support, then the underlying design principles can be reasonably expected to support independent learning in other settings as well. If print materials do not work well for distance learners, perhaps it is time to take a look at the operating assumptions behind the design.

Here are some guidelines that experienced practitioners use when they develop printed learning materials for conveying ideas and information. These guidelines are framed by the balance between theoretical and practical concepts in the content, the specific needs of the learners, and the learning context. They address presentation style, layout, use of illustrations and visual cues, and strategies for enabling learner participation.

When print is used to present theoretical conceptual material, the challenge is to engage the readers in more abstract thinking, to enable them to follow an argument and participate in the line of thought for themselves.

Presentation Style. The presentation style includes the writing style, the choice of language, and the approach to the learner. Print materials that address learners from afar and from on high make it more difficult for them to connect with either the material or its originator. Some authors believe that by encasing learning materials in the advanced language of their discipline, they are helping students to acquire essential academic reading skills, but experience from open and distance learning indicates that this is not the case. It is far more helpful to use a simple writing style that gradually eases the learner into the sequence of ideas and the language of the field. Practical strategies include organizing the material into manageable sections, providing short outlines for each chapter or section, and using titles, subtitles, and summaries that collectively provide a thread through the content (Misanchuk, 1992; Zubot, 1993).

As well, many authors use different voices throughout the materials, comparable to the different instructional stances used in the classroom. These voices can include that of the presenter of content, the tutor who helps learners develop learning skills and clarify the content for themselves, and the adviser who helps learners to work with the content and addresses any difficulties they have with the material. So, for example, the tutor voice lists the learning objectives, the presenter voice provides a coherent set of concepts, the tutor voice comes in again to ask learners how they relate these concepts to other aspects of the material, and the adviser voice suggests that learners respond to some questions and write down their own summary of the material. Although the process of planning a learning experience is much more conscious in print than in the classroom, there are many parallels. In fact, many instructors report that the experience of writing open and distance learning materials challenges them to develop a clearer writing style, improve their organization of the content, and consider how the learner would receive and use the material. These practices, in turn, improve their instructional strategies in the classroom.

So far, we have considered the use of print for presenting theoretical information in learning materials. But a great deal of learning entails combining theoretical concepts with a practical application—this multidimensional learning takes place in many sciences, and in medical, professional, and technical training. In this situation, it is equally essential that learners understand the underlying theoretical principles and its practical application. For example, technology students need to comprehend the basic physics principles of hydraulics and also need to know how these principles are applied in a hydraulic pump. The requirement that learners develop both a theoretical and a practical understanding adds another dimension to the learning experience and makes additional demands on the materials.

Learners need to be engaged intellectually and perceptually so that they can visualize and comprehend the processes being described and understand the underlying concepts. It helps to use several different strategies to present the same content so that learners are able to see it from different perspectives and select the approach that best suits their learning style. Examples, analogies, and repetition support a more three-dimensional approach to the material. The presenter voice in this situation is not that of a lecturer but of a guide who wants to be sure that learners notice everything that is to be observed, and the tutor voice provides alternative explanations in response to anticipated puzzlement and questions.

Layout. Layout—the way that words and images are presented on the page—can make the difference between learning materials that are accessible and materials that are frustrating to use. As with the presentation style, simplicity and openness are important features in layout of learning materials. Sometimes graphic designers want to introduce stylish elements, but the guiding principle for layout and design must be to make the material as usable as possible for the learner. Rather than distracting the learner by drawing attention to itself, the graphic design should provide an almost invisible support structure for the material and a clear path for the learner.

In practical terms, this means clearly delineating chunks of material, leaving open space on the page to provide a visual pathway and room for the learner to make notes, and ensuring that titles and subtitles are sufficiently notable that they offer a visual as well as a conceptual link. Many print materials also use icons, small graphics that provide consistent cues to the learner—for example, a book image to indicate that learners should complete a text reading at that point, or a coffee cup to suggest it is time to take a break. Icons can be effective if used judiciously to provide occasional graphic cues, but they can be distracting if they clutter the page with symbols that are not immediately recognizable.

Use of Illustrations and Visual Cues. Words are the primary vehicle for conveying theoretical concepts, but even in the theoretical domain, illustrations, charts, or graphs can be used effectively to enhance the printed text. Some theoretical content can be clarified by describing it visually—for example, using charts or graphs to demonstrate relationships between concepts, such as cause and effect, or to illustrate historical sequences. Images can also make the material more accessible to learners with a more visual orientation. An important guiding principle is to keep images as simple and as clear as possible without shortchanging the concepts being presented. Adding shading, color, or extraneous text can obscure the essential elements so that it is much harder for the learner to get the point.

Instructional material that contains a great deal of explanation and description depends far more on visual elements than theoretical content does. Usually, diagrams, drawings, and charts are used extensively, and the layout has to accommodate an effective combination of text and graphics so that the learner can readily connect the verbal explanations and pictorial descriptions.

Strategies for Enabling Learner Participation. Despite the use of different presentation voices, printed text can seem very one-sided. Well-designed learning materials have to include ways of letting learners in, enabling them to be active participants in a dialogue rather than passive recipients of content. This can be achieved through approaches that recognize that the learner is "there." One strategy is to address the learner directly from time to time. One very creative example was in a distance education women's studies course in which the course author, about a third of the way into the course, directly addressed the learners, in words to this effect, "Perhaps by now . . . you're really annoyed with the way I've presented things. That's fine. If you are, write me a letter and tell me why you disagree. I promise I'll consider your response seriously and will reply to it." In effect, this message indicated to learners that they were part of a dialogue; it gave them permission to disagree and recognized that learners were entitled to present their own responses to what was clearly a strong perspective.

Another way of letting the learners in is to provide regular opportunities for them to respond. These may range in structure and formality, from regular self-assessment questions to open-ended invitations to the learner to jot down thoughts that are evoked by the material. The print input can also be designed as a springboard for dialogue with the instructor and other learners, by prompting the learners to respond to the material and express their own ideas. If learners can use rapid communications technologies, such as e-mail and fax, to contribute to a discussion stimulated by reading print materials, they can take advantage of the durability and portability of print while making the best use of communications technology for interaction (O'Rourke, 1999).

Learning with Print

Both within and beyond academic situations, print instructional materials are used extensively as a learning companion. This genre of instructional materials includes how-to books, guides, and manuals. Browsing in airport bookstores may give the impression that this genre is a recent phenomenon, but in fact it has a long tradition that flourished with the nineteenth-century passion for practical knowledge, increased literacy, and rapid expansion of printing and publishing. Pitman's instruction in shorthand and Mrs. Beeton's guides to cookery and home management are examples of very successful print learning companions.

In the twenty-first century, the continued popularity of this type of print learning materials, despite the attraction of electronic media, shows that it effectively meets a demand for practical, accessible information. The portability of print makes it a preferred medium for how-to books for many hands-on tasks; it is much easier to carry a book into the garden or workshop than it is to carry a computer. Many popular books on practical topics use effective strategies that serve learners well and can provide a model for teaching materials used in more formal education settings. Usually, there are step-by-step descriptions well supported by illustrations, and the writing style is simple without being patronizing and incorporates a tone of encouragement, letting readers know that the task at hand is well within their capabilities. Very often, there are examples and anecdotes from the writer's personal experience, which serve to acknowledge that there is an emotional dimension to learning, even when it entails mastering a practical skill.

In formal education, the print learning companion sometimes takes on a more authoritarian approach, as in the highly structured competency-based learning materials that require learners to follow a specific pattern and complete tasks successfully before proceeding to the next section. Although these materials have been used extensively for skills development, many of them require the learner to follow a linear channeled approach that is not necessarily a good match for every learning style or learning context. The development of electronic learning materials that can accommodate multiple pathways to skills acquisition has the potential to change the shape of print-based skills training by prompting new approaches to creating multidimensional print materials. In contrast, the appeal of new electronic media could lead to an unproven assumption that print competency-based materials are necessarily more linear and limited than other media, and curtail the growth of print as a skills-training medium.

Learning Beside Print

One of the most important features of print as a learning resource is that learners can use it as a tool for their own self-expression. Moreover, the simplicity of print as a tool means that learners can concentrate on expressing their ideas rather than on the complex technical tasks of handling the medium.

Well-designed print instructional materials make it seem easy to respond. The compelling idea or the conversational tone prompts learners to want to have their say. As mentioned earlier, electronic media can be very useful in enabling learners to respond immediately and to interact with others, but there are also many situations where learners need to record for themselves each stage of their thinking, to develop their responses over time, and to rehearse ideas before sharing them with others. In a variation of the much-quoted "How do I know what I'm thinking until I hear what I have to say?" many learners write down their ideas as the first stage of finding out what they are thinking and what they will eventually want to say. Print captures ideas as they evolve over time and enables learners to reflect back on the process of learning and the stages of their own development. Although computers are a very convenient means of writing, they tend to collapse the time dimension by prompting us to eliminate previous versions of our work. This in turn mitigates against retrospective reflection that is an essential element of learning.

Some print materials are structured to enable learners to respond within the text, by answering questions or making notes. Learners can be encouraged to express their ideas in a written dialogue with the ideas presented in the materials; they can be guided through this process by means of suggested tasks or by prompts to consider a specific issue and then write their response to it in their learning journals. Development of good writing skills is an important aspect of all academic learning and of most areas of practical training, and print is still the basic medium of written expression, even when computers are used for production and transmission of written work. Well-written print material shows learners that good writing leads to clearer understanding of the writer's intent and provides models of effective writing styles that learners can adapt for their own work.

In the classroom, new approaches to print development are being used to enable learners, who previously faced formidable barriers, to gain expressive language. One example is BoardMaker, computer software that can be used to support children with disabilities such as autism or deafness as they develop images and graphics that speak for them when they cannot speak directly. The program can produce easily recognizable print drawings with the associated words or phrases that, for example, enable a child without spoken language to tell his classmates what he did during the past weekend. In addition, the program can be used as a support to a multimedia resource with voice output that allows children with limited or no spoken language to link words and ideas and develop other areas of language skills and literacy (Arlene Zuckernick, personal communication with the author, March 2000).

New Directions

Each new technology changes the previous technology (McLuhan, 1964). In the nineteenth century, photography liberated painting so that it moved beyond its role as a representational medium into impressionism, expressionism, and the whole domain of abstract art. But despite predictions of its demise, representational painting is still a very significant component of visual art. In the same way, electronic communications media can liberate print, and this does not necessarily mean that print will be diminished or even displaced from its traditional roles. Instead, it seems that the possibilities of print will expand as experimentation with electronic communications prompts us to reconsider the multidimensional potential of print.

A recent Canadian pilot project to provide Web-based literacy learning for adults illustrates how new media can lead to considering new ways of using old media. The AlphaRoute project developed Web-based literacy materials to be used by individual learners in local learning resource centers. Created to serve a range of learners, from minimally literate to mid-secondary school level, the program covered basic language content, such as vocabulary, grammar, and usage, as well as everyday life issues, such as health, employment, and leisure activities. The site was designed to enable learners to weave in their own life experience, to select content appropriate for their own skill level and interest, and to decide whether and how to work with others. The development team included adult basic educators and instructional designers who shared values about learner independence and curriculum relevance, although the former were generally rather wary of technology and the latter were new to the multiple dimensions of supporting literacy learners. During the development stage, discussions among the development team highlighted a number of issues about content and process in literacy learning, and raised questions about the extent to which the instructional strategies used for the multimedia materials might have been explored for print materials, if the print medium could have attracted the same degree of attention and external financing. The process of using the new media undoubtedly stimulated creative thinking about new ways of doing things, but as some team members pointed out there was no reason why this creative energy could not spill over into rethinking how familiar media could be used (Larocque, 2000).

Many opportunities exist for applying the well-tested principles of print design to the newer media. Cranford Teague (1999) deplores the sameness of type fonts used for Web sites and identifies technical strategies for expanding the range of available fonts. But he also points out that until the organizational issues of system compatibility and font designers' rights are resolved, Web sites will be afflicted with a visual monotony of type styles that would be unacceptable in conventional print materials.

The expanded use of computer-based media has drawn many more people to the written word as a means of communication and information gathering. Even though visual and sound elements are used to add dazzle to Web sites, the most frequent household use of the Internet is to obtain text-based information (Dickinson and Ellison, 1999). Web users are developing skills in finding information for themselves by following text-based cues and links, rather than passively accepting information delivered to them by television. Preliminary data suggest that regular Internet users have reduced the amount of time they spend watching television. It is hard to imagine that this dramatically increased access to written communication in electronic form will not also expand the use of written communication in permanent form—that is, in print. Although a great deal of Web use might be classified as entertainment or news gathering, a significant proportion can be described as informal learning, seeking information and answers to meet people's own defined learning needs, in the same way that they have used libraries or encyclopedias. The expanded opportunities for self-directed learning through electronic forms promise to stimulate learning from other media as well. The success of book selling over the Web offers a metaphor for how new media can actually promote interest in an old medium—print.

In the majority world, where few people have access to new computer media, print continues to be the essential instructional resource. It is unlikely that it will be feasible to use advanced computer communications for wide-scale education in the majority world in the immediate future. Lack of access to technology is generally regarded as a disadvantage, but this situation can also be an opportunity to preserve a degree of autonomy and integrity in the development and use of learning materials for education and training. Electronic media have the capacity to penetrate national borders and to overwhelm local cultures (Barlow, 2000). As long as print-based learning materials predominate in a region, it is possible to develop and use resources that are appropriate for local use and in keeping with regional cultural values. For the 80 percent of the world population that cannot afford to develop the required infrastructure for electronic media, there is still time to develop effective print-based learning resources that meet local needs before the educational media multinationals bring in their wares. The technology disparity can shelter the development of local learning resources, as long as funding is made available for old technologies as well as for accessible new technologies. The significant inequity in access to new technologies makes the older technologies, such as print, even more important.

In summary, print is a durable and robust medium that supports learning because it enables us to take in knowledge from any era and to process it in our own time and space. Well-designed print materials allow us to choose the pace, direction, and contours of our learning.

References

Barlow, M. "The WTO Services Negotiations and the Threat to Canada's Public Health and Education Systems." 2000. [www.canadians.org/publications/speech].

Bates, A. W. *Technology, Open Learning, and Distance Education.* New York: Routledge, 1995.

Cranford Teague, J. "The Times (and Helvetica), They Are A'Changin'." *The Independent,* Oct. 4, 1999, p. 15.

Dickinson, P., and Ellison, J. "Plugged into the Internet." *Canadian Social Trends,* 55. Ottawa, Ontario: Statistics Canada, 1999.

Friere, P. *Education for a Critical Consciousness.* New York: Continuum, 1983.

Iser, W. *The Act of Reading.* London: Routledge & Kegan Paul, 1978.

Larocque, D. "Research Report on the Alpharoute Project." 2000. [http://village.ca/eng/projects/Alpha2_english.pdf].

McLuhan, H. M. *Understanding Media.* New York: New American Library, 1964.

Misanchuk, E. *Preparing Instructional Text: Document Design Using Desktop Publishing.* Englewood Cliffs, N.J.: Educational Technology Publications, 1992.

O'Rourke, J. "From Course in a Box to Course on a Stick: Adventures in Open and Distance Learning." Collected conference papers, Cambridge International Conference on Open and Distance Learning, 1999. Cambridge, U.K.: Open University, 1999.

Zubot, M. *Writing Your Course: A Short Guide for Writers of Distance Education Materials.* Saskatoon: University Extension Press, University of Saskatchewan, 1993.

JENNIFER O'ROURKE *is an educational consultant in open and distance learning and is based at Gabriola Island, British Columbia, Canada.*

6

A recent initiative in educational radio successfully used a new design—a doculecture—to attract credit learners and interested members of the public.

Radio as a Learning Technology

May Maskow

Educational radio refers here to broadcasts designed to inform the public and at the same time carry the major content of formal university credit courses delivered through distance education. Radio is used widely as a distance education technology in countries that have large student bodies but inadequate traditional infrastructures to serve them, such as South Africa and China. Elsewhere, radio's popularity as a learning technology varies from country to country. Educational radio is relatively unused in North America. It was initiated, then abandoned in the United States in the early days of public radio (Pittman, 1986). Between the two world wars, leading educators believed that radio would radically transform American higher education. They soon changed their minds; trend-setting University of Iowa's inaugural educational broadcasts in 1924, for example, brought complaints of "boring, lackluster programming." Its more course-centered radio programs of 1926 drew a rash of interest from students, but by 1932 these broadcasts had vanished for reasons including scant broadcast parts of the courses, little interest from faculty in lecturing on radio, an undefined population of potential students, and not enough recognition from the members of the public of their need for ongoing formal learning (Pittman, 1986). By 1940 educational radio in higher education in North America was history.

The same reasons Pittman found for the failure of educational radio in the 1920s would cause failure today, except perhaps for the now-increased public perception of the need for formal education. Open College in Toronto, Canada, addressed these and other issues over the last thirty years and made an audio-based distance education initiative thrive. In a collaboration between CJRT-FM and Ryerson Polytechnic University, adult students could take university credit courses on the air as only a small part of a weekly public audience that grew to fifty thousand listeners per week. I believe that what was learned in the process could lead to a resurgence of radio as a learning technology. In this chapter I will outline highlights of Open College work as they relate to quality assurance for educational radio. But first, some background.

The Widespread Use of Radio

Radio is almost universally available. Radio Advertising Bureau (2000) data show that in the United States radio reaches 95.3 percent of the population twelve years of age and over, and they listen on average for 21.7 hours per week. As for where people listen, 41.6 percent are in the car, 36.7 percent are at home, and 21.7 percent are at work. Internet users listen often to radio: 87.4 percent who are online for three hours or more a week tune in.

In the seventies, the availability of radio expanded significantly with the widespread use of the audiocassette. It was inexpensive, radio programs were easy to copy, and audio players rapidly became standard equipment in automobiles and homes. With the introduction of the Sony Walkman in 1980, radio became available at any time and in any place. Now we listen to recordings of radio programs on compact disk and the Internet.

How we listen to radio is an important point. Some radio listening is background to our performance of tasks that require concentration. Other listening is foreground, the radio we concentrate on while carrying out the habitual and mundane tasks of everyday living. Radio producers are conscious of producing programs as either background or foreground, but whether radio is received as background or foreground depends on the choice of the listener. Educational radio is unequivocally produced as foreground.

Radio's Place in Education: Assets and Limitations

The human voice creates a powerful presence with which a listener may identify. Voiced words convey attitude, emotion, color, and energy (Burge, Norquay, Roberts, and Toppings, 1987); they also can convince, persuade, excite the imagination, and contextualize difficult concepts. On radio a teacher can persuade a learner to search out information, evaluate perspectives, and contemplate alternatives or to assess outcomes and reflect on judgments. A radio voice can support the kinds of learning that require the listener to think, question, analyze, and develop conceptual frameworks. In contrast, radio is not a good medium for the kinds of learning that require visual stimulation; when the learner must observe, calculate, graph, or quantify, just about any other learning technology is better. Open College staff has found that radio is well suited as a learning technology for formal courses in history, poetry, comparative literature, and some social sciences, but it is unsuitable for teaching science, mathematics, or art history.

Educational Radio's Reawakening in North America

In 1971, just after the Open University in the United Kingdom was established, Ryerson Polytechnical Institute (now Ryerson Polytechnic University) in Toronto owned CJRT-FM, Canada's first noncommercial FM radio station. As an experiment that year, sociology professor and broadcaster Margaret Norquay (1993) used the station to teach an introductory sociology course to adults. With this single event, educational radio resurfaced in North America and both a learning technology and Open College emerged. (It was called "open" because students could register for a course with no entrance requirements: a radical idea in Canada then.)

In teaching terms, the first Open College radio programs reflected what went on in a university classroom: an on-air lecture, course arrangements such as assignments, and examination preparation. But there was one significant difference: each program ended with a twenty-minute interview with a sociology expert because Norquay knew that interviews made good radio. More courses followed, with each one including twenty-four one-hour radio programs, an on-campus orientation, and a weekend face-to-face seminar at Ryerson. Students received specially designed materials, used the telephone to talk with their assigned tutor, and wrote essays and a final examination to at least the same academic standard as for on-campus students.

By the mid-1980s CJRT-FM had become a nonprofit, noncommercial station independent from Ryerson. Its financial support came from listeners, corporate donations, and a grant from the provincial government. In 1986 CJRT-FM became available on cable via satellite throughout Ontario. Open College course broadcasts became available also on audiocassette. Student enrollment grew as the courses attracted a wide variety of adults in small and large towns (Paddy, 1989). One significant problem emerged, however: the radio station personnel did not approve of the quality of Open College broadcasts. Although they were effective in educational terms, they were not good enough to match the other programming in the station's mass market. Change was needed if Open College was to remain on the air.

Adaptations to Make Educational Radio Interesting to Listeners. Course-related items that did not affect the general public were removed and placed into accompanying print materials. The number of one-hour programs per course was reduced to twelve.

On comparing the sound of Open College courses with programs hosted by professional broadcasters, Open College staff realized that some professors had voices that created listening problems; for example, they were monotonic and felt "flat." In response, criteria were developed for selecting a professor to teach on radio: sound academic credentials, teaching experience, a wide range of contacts in the professor's field of expertise, and a "radio trainable" voice. Only the first three were relatively easy to assess, so to determine whether a professor had a voice that could be trained for broadcasting the staff designed an innovative four-step audition process. *Step 1:* An applicant with the appropriate credentials was invited to write and record a radio script and to prepare and conduct an interview with an expert colleague. *Step 2:* The Open College production team evaluated these recordings by listening to them without meeting the candidate—all they heard was the recorded voice, just as would an ordinary listener. *Step 3:* If the team judged that the professor had the potential to be trained as a broadcaster, the candidate was invited to work with a producer to prepare a half-hour pilot program. *Step 4:* The decision about whether the professor indeed had a voice suitable for training was made on the basis of the recorded script, the interview, and the pilot program. Preparing the pilot program had a further advantage; it acquainted the aspiring distance mode professor with the type and amount of work involved in preparing a course for radio.

Developing the Doculecture. The most significant analysis of early Open College programming activity revealed the importance of the interview. It not only was the most interesting and "listenable" part of an Open College program but also gave scope for making a program more learner-centered because it mentally engaged the listener-learner in the professor's questions and the experts' responses. This type of engagement suggested that the radio documentary was the format needed. Expert practitioners anywhere in the world could explain their practice and academic researchers could discuss their latest investigations, with both groups being able to interpret the significance of their work and answer questions posed by the professor to obtain information, draw analyses, challenge values, and help the learner to think critically. Questions and answers are a form of mental gymnastics that can bring about the interpretation and evaluation of concepts, so Open College professors were deliberately trained to pose critical rather than interrogative questions.

A technical reason also showed why the interview (as opposed to a lecture) works particularly well on radio. As the early pioneers in radio learned, after a short time a single voice sounds monotonous in audio terms and boring in psychological terms. The listener mentally tunes out and turns the radio off or tunes in to another station—a most undesirable situation for a broadcaster.

The potential for producing informative, engaging, and even provocative radio documentary programs is vast. Although a radio producer and investigative reporter can draw from documented information, take a particular perspective, or pursue an original line of inquiry to create a lively story for the general public, an academic course is more prescribed and bound by a course outline approved by an accrediting body. It was found that well-selected and approved academic courses suitable for radio could be produced in documentary format that would also interest large numbers of the listening public. Open College professors were well aware that their goal was to seek out and interpret research-based knowledge and that each program was based on a set of clear student-centered learning objectives.

Training Professors for Doculectures. Radio scripts are written for the ear so that when read aloud they sound as if the speaker is intimately addressing only one person, the listener. This style is quite different from academic writing for the eye. Before training began, therefore, the professor was given two in-house publications (McLaughlin, 1986; Toppings, 1995) and assigned a producer. This person's role was technical and editorial with the degree of editorial control varying from one assignment to another. The producer recorded and edited interviews, edited the professor's scripts, directed the script reading, and assembled the whole program. The professor maintained consistent editorial control of the academic content. Meanwhile, a voice coach gave the professor initial voice training followed by further direction by the producer as scripts were read. At its completion, but before going on air, each program was evaluated by an outside consultant and reviewed by the Open College director. The consultant's written evaluation was given to the producer and professor and any necessary changes made. Such rigorous, continual evaluation worked well: professors commented on their enhanced teaching skills, and others cited it as one of the factors responsible for the steady improvement of Open College.

Attracting Academic Experts and Teaching Professors. As its reputation grew, Open College attracted more distinguished senior professors from universities in and close to Toronto, most of whom prepared their courses while on sabbatical leave. Professors hired by Open College interviewed guest experts in the CJRT studios and also recorded interviews face-to-face with colleagues (for example, at conferences) and by telephone to remote locations, usually a campus radio station. If there was no campus station at an American university, arrangements were made to record the expert at a local public broadcasting station. Recordings of the conversation were made at both ends and spliced together for editing. One Open College course could contain interviews with as many as fifty different experts. Professors sometimes engaged in a game with themselves and each other to see how many academic "stars" they could interview for their programs. An economist, for example, was successful in interviewing six Nobel laureates for her course, whereas another professor teaching a course on the history of espionage obtained interviews with KGB and CIA agents and former British Intelligence officers as well as the expected historians and researchers. The professor of a course on the history of Canada and Quebec (broadcast at campus stations across Canada just prior to the 1995 Quebec referendum on its sovereignty) interviewed prominent historians, journalists, and politicians, including the Prime Minister of Canada. It is no surprise that professors went to such lengths for their programs: with listening audiences in the thousands and much interest from their peers they could exert considerable intellectual influence.

Extending the Reach of Open College Courses. During the past five years, Open College has attracted on average fifty thousand listeners a week, according to Bureau of Broadcast Management data. As well as being aired on campus stations, Open College courses are leased by distance education universities (such as Athabasca University in Alberta and the Open Learning Agency in British Columbia) to mix audio into their distance education technologies or gain an extra alternative to hiring staff when they lack the in-house expertise to develop a needed course. Each week the other non-commercial radio station in Canada, CKUA-AM-FM in Alberta, broadcasts the audio portion of one of the courses leased by its partner, Athabasca University.

Audio Distance Education on the Internet. In 1998, in cooperation with York University and Industry Canada, Open College put four audio-based courses onto the Internet. The audio was available to the student by password at any time, and no transcription appeared on the screen. Instead, students typed notes or participated in other course activities while listening to the audio. They could also engage in online discussions with classmates and their tutors. One feature, unique to the doculecture course, was the invitation to one or more of the interviewed experts to join weekly online synchronous or asynchronous chats with the professor, tutor and learners. Experimentation continues with this form of delivery.

Planning Issues

Before beginning an educational radio initiative, adult educators need to consider four issues. First, they need to plan how to market to learners who would benefit especially from using radio as a medium for their continuing education. Second, they need to determine at the outset the ownership of editorial control of course production and course content. Third, they must decide who pays for the cost of course development and radio production and in what proportion. Fourth, they must establish intellectual property rights.

Marketing Educational Radio to Adult Learners. Open College students coupled two features of audio and found time efficiency and flexibility—both precious commodities in their busy lives. Radio as foreground can engage the thinking mind while the learner performs habitual or automatic psychomotor routines. Flexibility functions in time and location. An audiocassette version of the radio broadcast can be played anytime and anywhere. For example, students have said that they listen to their course work while driving to work or while sitting on a bus or plane. Many have said their family, home, and work responsibilities left little time for study so they could not have taken these courses if it were not for the listening flexibility feature. These reactions have been used to promote Open College to single parents, shift workers, and time-strapped professionals, thus finding a niche market of appreciative learners.

Determining Editorial Control of Production. At play here is the delicate and complex interaction between the producer-broadcaster of radio programs, the professor who prepares them, and the academic institution, which credits and delivers the courses.

If the production of a course is done in a radio station and a radio producer has editorial control of the content of a program—as is often the practice in the production of general radio documentaries—there may be the temptation to overemphasize facts or exploit a questionable point to make a program more interesting to the listener. But if this practice is transferred to a credit course, academic integrity is compromised. In contrast, when an academic institution is the producer, there is the danger that the broadcasting partner may find the quality of production inadequate to satisfy a mass market. If these differing standards are recognized prior to entering into a partnership, policies and procedures can be developed to prevent controversies over the editorial control of course content and the responsibility for production. Distance education by radio usually has two collaborating partners; whether these are a university and radio station or a department of education and broadcasting authority, the partners have different organizational cultures that can create difficulties in the most significant part of the collaborative process, that is, standard setting.

Deciding Who Pays. Quality-assured educational radio courses are more costly to produce than those designed for print, audioconferencing, or the World Wide Web (in my experience). When educational material is broadcast on a mass medium its cost cannot be supported by the usual funding parties, and certainly not by the fees paid by registered students. At issue therefore is how much funding comes from the mass market, who in the mass market pays, and who makes the decisions about shared costs. The decision maker or decision makers could be government, a broadcasting authority, a radio station, or an academic institution. Funding can come from advertisers, from donations by corporations and foundations, and from contributions by listeners. No matter who contributes, it is important to decide at the beginning of the collaboration how the funding will work. It is also helpful to recognize ahead of time that difficulties can arise if funding sources change. Open College received support from government, foundations, and listeners, but difficulties recently arose when government funding was abruptly withdrawn as part of draconian cuts across all education sectors. Open College had to reconfigure its financing.

Establishing Intellectual Property Rights. This complex issue needs attention in the earliest planning stages, especially in terms of who owns the rights to broadcasts, interviews, and written materials, and to courses put on the Internet. Legal advice is imperative.

Future Directions

As radio becomes digital (for recording, editing, transmission, and also receiving) and expands its presence on the Internet, the listener gets better-quality sound, greater choice of programs, and greater flexibility in listening opportunities. Although radio on the Internet is expanding some markets into a global sphere, its low cost is spawning small, specialized stations directed to new or specialized interests. Some long-established broadcasters extend their reach by making themselves available on the Internet (Lavers, 1999), while new stations available only on the Internet add to the competition. Furthermore, governments are changing their broadcast policies. As the changes settle somewhat, I believe there will be a great demand for content directed to niche markets, two being formal and informal adult and continuing education. Commercial producers likely will compete with academic institutions for this market. So let us look at four scenarios.

Scenario 1: Traditional public broadcasters could reinvent educational radio by collaborating with universities to develop radio that appeals to their credit students and at the same time expand opportunities for adult potential learners. Public radio provides high-quality talk with excellent networked documentary programs, which challenge and broaden the mind, but it has not seriously ventured into formal distance education. The forthcoming generations of adults who recognize their need for continuing education but need flexibility and mobility in its delivery could bring new interest and new support to public radio. From a university's perspective, collaborating with public radio to showcase some of its continuing education offerings in the doculecture format may help illustrate and expand public interest in the work of university teachers and researchers. Appropriately designed and produced, the programs could appeal to alumni and corporations who support the university and to listeners who support public radio.

Scenario 2: In developing countries technological developments in broadcasting and listening are creating new opportunities for very small communities. The Commonwealth of Learning (1998) reports that for less than $1,000 (U.S.) a portable low-powered FM radio broadcasting station with a range of ten kilometers in all directions can be transported in a large briefcase to a village and made fully operational in just half a day. This unit has a transmitter, small mixer, microphone, and pairs of CD and cassette players. Although it is used primarily for community development, many adult educators see it playing a larger role in informal and formal education. Also available is a sturdy windup radio that uses muscle power and solar energy instead of electricity or batteries. This portable receiver is useful in nonwalled learning settings; for example, a group of teenagers can gather around a tree with a radio slung over it. In developing countries where student numbers have increased but the infrastructures and numbers of trained teachers have not, the potential for educational radio is significant.

Scenario 3: Two digital satellite radio services, Sirius Satellite Radio (www.cdradio.com) and XM Satellite Radio (www.armc.com), designed specifically for vehicles, will be introduced in the United States in early 2001. Each will deliver up to one hundred channels of entertainment programming targeted to motorists for certain subscriber and monthly fees. Digital sound is clear, and when transmitted by satellite the same radio station will be heard at the same time throughout North America. I see distance education for all kinds of communities as a potential market for these satellite radio services.

Scenario 4: Radio stations from large government stations to small privately owned ones from all over the world now use the Internet. Such radio stations place information and advertising on their Web sites. It is also relatively easy, inexpensive, and regulation-free to set up radio that broadcasts only through the Internet. Because such Internet radio stations have some interactive capacity there is real potential for them to sustain structured group work and informal learning dialogue. Furthermore, a technology being developed for a wide market makes it possible to take audio data from the Internet and listen to it anytime and anyplace, thus enhancing mobile studying. Internet radio will also be more accessible at home. Without the aid of a computer, a stand-alone radio receiver with a power outlet and phone line equipped with an Internet connection will offer AM-FM and Internet stations plus a catalogue of radio programs (www.kerbango.com).

Although the preceding are all potential scenarios, the hard wave technology that plays a major role in shaping these futures is changing so rapidly that it is difficult to predict with any certainty just what role educational radio will play. Another factor, and a conundrum of radio recognized by the industry yet rarely articulated elsewhere, is the vast difference in the cost of producing intelligent, reflective radio compared with the cost of spinning records for background listening. Market forces, particularly in North America, propel radio; advertisers sponsor programs and advertising is sold on the basis of mass ratings. Educational radio that attracts small target audiences rather than a mass audience is more difficult to market; although it is not as costly as most documentaries and can have a longer shelf life, its production cost still places it in a limited market. Finally, many members of the listening public have experienced little educational radio, so the idea is still new to many, making it difficult to market. Nevertheless, the idea of taking a course on the Internet was unheard of just a few years ago. Based on the Open College case study, if distance education via quality educational radio becomes more popular, it will likely profile the work of outstanding professors who bring an international focus to their teaching. Above all, although radio as a technology may be ubiquitous, it needs a certain mix of professional skills to render it a successful learning technology.

References

Burge, L., Norquay, M., Roberts, J., and Toppings, E. *Listening to Learn: The Use of Voice in Distance Education.* Toronto, Ontario: Ontario Institute for Studies in Education, 1987.

Commonwealth of Learning. "Technology Renewal." *Connections,* 1998, 3(2), 1. [www.col.org/connlink.htm]

Lavers, D. "Internet Radio." *Broadcast Dialogue,* 1999, Mar. 25–43.

McLaughlin, P. *How to Interview: The Art of the Media Interview.* North Vancouver, Canada: Self-Counsel Press, 1986.

Norquay, M. "Personal Reflections on the Early Years of Ryerson Open College." *Journal of Distance Education,* 1993, *8*(1), 71–83.

Paddy, V. "University of the Air." *The Review Imperial Oil Limited,* 1989, *71*(3), 13–17.

Pittman, V. Jr. "Station WSUV and the Early Days of Instructional Radio." *The Palimpsest,* 1986, *45*(3), 38–52.

Radio Advertising Bureau. *Radio Marketing and Fact Book for Advertisers, Fall 1999 to Spring, 2000.* New York: Radio Advertising Bureau, 1999. [www.rab.com]

Toppings, E. *Writing for Radio.* Toronto, Ontario: CJRT-FM, 1995.

MAY MASKOW was the director of Open College at CJRT-FM for eleven years and also director of media education at Ryerson Polytechnic University. She is now president of Doculec Productions.

7

To help adult educators adopt the new technologies, their approaches to teaching and learning must be assessed. Wise professional developers who know the key issues and strategies can help them accept and use new learning technologies.

Professional Development for Web-Based Teaching: Overcoming Innocence and Resistance

Genevieve M. Gallant

"Not many people undertaking mountaineering for the first time would attempt to climb Everest on the first day. Yet many educators acquire some conferencing software and then try and design and run some kind of pilot online course. When their experiment fails, they rarely blame themselves, often stating that the medium is not very suitable for learning" (Prendergast, 2000, p. 294).

"Our networked activities are not viewed as an external intervention but as a local closed forum for the issues staff are experiencing, rooted in real local examples, restricted to small groups with similar training needs to provide the safe environment in which sharing can occur" (Tickner, 2000, p. 334).

Between these two situations there is a world of difference. Each one illustrates how teachers may approach—by default or design—developing their teaching skills for using new learning technologies. The development-by-default route, and other routes where development paths are not carefully designed, may lead to many institutional, teaching, and learning problems. (As Wills and Alexander, 2000, show in a list of sixteen course development project failures, for example.) The development-by-design route may lead to enhanced teaching skills and learning outcomes as, for example, is shown in Frayer's case study of Duquesne University (1999).

Which developmental route to take and which results to achieve are the key questions, so in this chapter I rely on my own experience and values as a professional developer, as well as some current literature, to outline key issues and principles for managing educators' innocence and resistance and ensuring that learning, not technology, drives decision making. The professional development issues discussed are adult educator change reactions and attributes of adoptable innovations, infrastructure support, and strategic planning. The professional development action principles discussed are responsiveness, continuity, community, and constructive activity. This chapter acts as a signpost to good planning; many details about specific skill enhancement activities can be found in the References at the end of the chapter.

Contextual Factors

First, it is worth mentioning two contextual factors, because they are part of the information-flooded environment in which busy teachers try to stay afloat. The first factor is the growing number of books and articles about the effects of technology in higher education and the lessons learned (Bates, 1999; Gillespie, 1998; Katz and Rudy, 1999) and the analyses of institutional transitions and change imperatives (Barr and Tagg, 1995; Evans and Nation, 2000; Oblinger and Rush, 1997). Teachers are already coping with changing student profiles, reduced resources, increased workloads, competition for research funds and enrollments, and verbalized expectations of service from a community to its educational agencies. When adopting learning technology is added to the mix, these stressors can overload everyone concerned.

The second contextual factor is the large amount of staff development and teaching skill development material now available in paper, at conferences, and electronically on the Web. Indeed, "large" understates the issue, even if we look only at Web-based teaching material. Since the earliest material on online teaching and learning was issued just over a decade ago, publishers now produce many books (Cahoon, 1998; Salmon, 2000) and professional staff development associations and other groups produce useful materials and conferences; for example, in the United States, the EDUCAUSE publications (www.educause.edu) and the American Association of Higher Education (www.aahe.org) and its affiliate the TLT Group (www.tltgroup.org); in the United Kingdom, the international conference Networked Lifelong Learning (Networked Learning 2000, held at Lancaster University) and the journal *Innovations in Education and Training International*; in Canada, the Society for Teaching and Learning in Higher Education (www.umanitoba.ca/academic_support/uts/stlhe) and an international conference specific to Web-based teaching and learning, NAWEB (www. unb.ca/wwwdev/); and in Australia, the conferences of the Higher Education Research and Development Society of Australasia (HERDSA; www. herdsa.org.au). Various helpful experts and offices compile Web-based gateways and material for their colleagues; for example, in the United Kingdom, Bostock's review Web site of virtual learning environments (www.seda.demon.co.uk/eddevs/virtlearn.html); in Canada, the federal government's Office of Learning Technologies (http://olt-bta.hrdc-drhc.gc.ca); in the United States, the University of Maryland University College (http://www. umuc.edu/distance/odell/cvu/); and in Australia, the University of New England style guide for online teaching materials (www.une.edu.au/online-info/ style/).

If these specialized sites were not enough, more information can be found in sites carrying broader information about teacher development. For example, one gateway, www.lgu.ac.uk/deliberations, gives links to no less than fifty-two general staff development journals, seventy-two subject-based journals, and forty-four staff development centers in U.K. universities. From there, an intrepid inquirer can go to international sites or seek out paper documents on staff development published by groups such as the Staff and Educational Development Association (SEDA) in the United Kingdom (www.seda.demon.co.uk), HERDSA, or the AAHE.

Professional Development Issues

Information about technology, institutional and personal change, and also staff development abounds, but how to synthesize and tailor it into effective professional development-by-design is the challenge. And underpinning that is the question of how professional development is conceptualized. Is it remedial or transformative, voluntary or mandated? How do we identify which actions will be relevant across a variety of busy professionals— or is that the wrong question? How might we dismantle at least some of the barriers to change? What kinds of support are most appropriate for sustainable adoption of learning technologies or changes in teaching style? There is no single best way to carry out professional development, but strategic thinking is necessary to achieve commonsense approaches and client-sensitive responsive behaviors. The first category of professional development issues therefore concerns differences in generic teacher reactions to change and the attributes of adoptable innovations.

Reactions to Change, Attributes of Adoptable Innovations. Educators of adults show their individuality in various ways, especially in how their own discipline conditions their thinking and behavior, how they teach, and how they react to innovation adoption. Here the work of Rogers (1995) is relevant because no professional developer can afford to miss the signals sent out by members of the different adopter categories regarding their attitude to innovation adoption. The *early adopters,* for example, may act as informed and respected opinion leaders because they experiment with an innovation to see how it might help the processes of teaching and learning (rather than merely to explore the intricacies of the software) and they are relatively free of the strong enthusiasm of the *innovators* (who eagerly test out any new product and take a product-oriented approach in that testing). Early adopters use their own professional networks to discuss their experience or show their more cautious colleagues the shortcuts and other strategies to smooth the path of innovation. Early adopters can greatly help the work of a professional developer who is trying to reach the *early majority*—that larger group that waits to a certain extent, although not as long as do the more skeptical and risk-averse *late majority*. The early majority people analyze the characteristics of various learning technologies against their teaching values and styles and think through various ethical, application, and workload issues before they decide to experiment and knowingly trade off some of the more challenging effects of the innovation against the less-challenging familiar or efficient old habits (Burge, 1999).

A wise professional development person will legitimize early-majority behaviors and attitudes and connect them to appropriate early adopters. The developer will help administrators guard against the innovators trying to command big chunks of resource budgets (with arguments often based on self-interest that continuous and immediate updating of software and hardware is imperative). The wise developer will tactfully manage any unproductive expressions of doubt or cynicism from the late majority—those who will adopt only much later, when they feel no risk at all, when very easy to use and reliable technology is ubiquitous, or when really pushed by peers or administrators. Best left alone are the *laggards*—who rely on tradition and habit and question the activities of anyone who promotes innovation adoption or works with the early majority (or, even worse, innovators). But if a university has a very articulate professor who publicly airs her or his concerns, documents actual examples of early adopter and early majority adoption failures or examples of impulsive thinking, and gains wide attention (Young, 2000), then the professional developer has to decide how much energy to spend on refuting or clarifying the laggard's claims.

Some colleagues (Fox and Herrmann, 2000; Thompson, 1999) have already formulated variations on these categories. For example, Fox and Herrmann refer to five categories of people's reactions to innovation: *neutral, booster, oppositional, skeptical,* and *transformational*. Thompson shows how the technological and educational cultures may clash to create adoption problems and demand the consequent interpretive, mediating, or even remedial attention of a staff developer: "Often, and sadly, the more developed and sophisticated the product the less effective the presentation will be, as what is demonstrated seems so remote from the real world experience of the [early or later majority adult educator]" (p. 154).

Rogers (1995) describes another useful generic concept: the attributes needed for an innovation to be adopted. An adult educator is more likely to adopt a new learning technology or a change in teaching method (not necessarily the same thing) if it has some or all of the following six attributes: relative advantage (for example, security, mobility, or efficiency) over existing methods; compatibility with existing contextual elements and dynamics; low levels of complexity in actual use; reliability over continual use; testability within existing practices and without great changes in the current modus operandi; and observability, that is, is easily seen by the early and late majority members. An experienced professional developer will consider how each attribute is valued and discussed by individual educators. The University of Washington's Catalyst Project (http://depts.washington. edu/catalyst/home.html and http://www.educause.edu/ir/library/html/ cem9934.html) is a good example. The university approached technology adoption by deliberately focusing attention on *mainstream pragmatists* (not the early adopters or even early majority) and therefore on "introducing innovation, rather than technology, into teaching and learning, and using the Web resources and Web-based services to diffuse innovations and provide technical support to faculty" (Donovan, 1999, p. 1).

Infrastructure Support. The qualities of the technological and operational support infrastructure of an institution are also an issue. The presence of a professional development center or a learning and teaching center (see the www.lgu.ac.uk/deliberations gateway for many Web addresses) is key. The center can communicate a vision of how and why changes are being planned or implemented, as well as ensure that changes are driven by learning and teaching issues rather than by "the imperatives of economic rationalism or the 'silicon veneer' of technological determinism" (Latchem and Lockwood, 1998, p. xx). Such centers may provide multiskilled teams to guide teachers in the development of learning materials and the use of new teaching technologies. Skills represented in such teams may include learning design, graphic design editing, multimedia production, evaluation, and e-librarianship. The use of these combined skills can help educators avoid the Everest situation (Prendergast, 2000) or project mismanagement, as in "a lone academic assuming a range of roles [and then having a project fail] because the particular academic simply did not have the time or expertise to carry out every role" (Wills and Alexander, 2000, p. 59).

A center or another service can also design and offer a smorgasbord of workshops and just-in-time (rather than just-in-case) assistance and training for teachers; that is, when, where, and why they need such help, at a level appropriate to their existing technical proficiency. The all-too-familiar computer technician or early adopter showing his level of digital expertise (often with some flourish of satisfaction) is often little appreciated by the adult educator who, uninterested in "bells and whistles" or arcane explanations, is looking for cognitive expertise to implement learning strategies (Olgren, this volume) or needs help with an operational procedure. The development center can provide help and advice when it suits the clients, rather than from 9 A.M. to 5 P.M. five days a week. Wise development staff would avoid simple, fast fix-it actions or any others that inhibit an adult educator's learning what is necessary for basic operation of software. It is far better to place the teacher gently in the role of adult learner, experiencing sound adult learning facilitation principles, as some educational leaders have suggested already (Frayer, 1999). "Staff should be able to put themselves in the learner's shoes and actively experience the learning environments that are advocated for their students" (Wills and Alexander, 2000, p. 65). The University of Strathclyde in Scotland does just that at its virtual university (http://cvu.strath.ac.uk).

Strategic Planning. Third, the institutional strategies for planning the management of technology-based change are also important. I highlight four key issues here: changes in teaching styles, rewards and incentives, ethical issues, and general strategic planning.

Changes in teaching style are to be expected when an adult educator learns about alternatives to the transmission model of teaching, recognizes the cognitive functions of learner-to-learner interaction and facilitator responsiveness, and sees the potential in old and new learning technologies for enhanced interaction and greater learner responsibility. The technology itself will never guarantee improved teaching and learning, as examples of just "throwing" lecture notes onto the Web have shown. What is needed instead is informed discussion about alternative educational paradigms (Barr and Tagg, 1995), how approaches such as constructivism can be applied (Jonassen, 1999; Wilson and Lowry, this volume), how a focus can be kept on learning strategies (Olgren, this volume) and information literacy (Kerka, this volume), how the adult educator's function may be changed but never diminished (often a secret fear to be addressed discreetly and immediately), and how a combination of learning technologies should serve learning and teaching without loss of academic rigor (another fear). The constructivist approach and all its methods can be used well with various technologies when each technology—be it print, audio, or computer conferencing—supports active learning and enables the teacher to act as a guiding partner. Because the initial teaching model of many adult educators comes from their own teachers (many of whom used teacher-centered strategies), it becomes quite a challenge for some of them to shift gears or indeed change vehicles altogether, adopt other models, and explore such things as experiential, problem-based, and collaborative learning models as well as how learning technologies may fit into those models. A related challenge comes in adapting to working in a course design or learning materials production team rather than following the traditional lone academic path.

Rewards and incentives for adult educators making significant changes in their teaching styles are therefore important, especially for the early adopters, the early majority, and the late majority groups. Change and development rarely happen to most adult educators unless they juggle workloads, face the aftereffects following a first encounter with a new object or event, even a seductive one (Khaslavsky and Shedroff, 1999), react to collegial cynicism or envy, take on extra work, or become overwhelmed by enthusiastic students embracing a new technology and expecting instant responses. That last issue is especially important for Web work. Teachers will continue to face such situations until they can redesign the learning processes or make the bigger shift from a teacher-centered view ("I have to answer all messages by default") to a learner-centered one ("Learners exchange messages by design"). Incentive strategies need to include a combination of public recognition (institutional, national awards), highest-level and articulated management support, tangible assistance (for example, just-in-time help as often as needed, a smorgasbord of workshops), formal release from regular teaching schedules to work with a course development team, and promotion criteria that take into account an adult educator's proven skills in new or expanded ways of teaching.

Ethical issues become evident in adopting a learning technology, and (in my experience) they tend to be analyzed at some length by the early and later majority adopters. Confidentiality, intellectual property ownership, power relationships, equality of access, psychological well-being, and plagiarism are already well outlined (Holt, 1998). An important point to make here, apart from stressing that management, professional developers, and adult educators themselves should openly explore all these issues at the earliest stages in Web work, is that learner privacy must be respected. Software permits tracking of log-ins, for example, but that facility is no excuse for a teacher's unannounced statistical monitoring activity.

The importance of institutionwide strategic planning cannot be underestimated (Latchem and Moran, 1998). At stake are its human, material, and financial resources, as well as its external reputation and its internal harmony. The widespread use of learning technologies brings infrastructure and human development needs. It produces effects (sometimes unexpected and unwelcome) in many areas of institutional practice, including library services, records and admissions procedures, and tutor training when the adult educator is not the sole teacher in a course. Planning is, of course, a matter for an individual institution, but external agencies or professional groups can assist. The Association of Canadian Community Colleges, for example, examined the effects of information technologies and found a need for widespread development of ordinary good teaching skills as well as for technological skills (http://www.acc.ca/english/forum/publications/technology.htm). Latchem and Moran (1998) provide many specific and sound guidelines for strategic planning.

With so many issues to manage, busy practitioners can benefit from a concise set of action principles for professional development.

Action Principles

Because many adult educators have little or no formal training in how to teach, even before they are faced with learning technology adoption it is reasonable to assume that any professional development activity should both treat them as adult learners and focus on the generics of effective teaching (Wills and Alexander, 2000)—especially how to promote interactivity that goes beyond merely asking questions from lecture notes. The key principles for doing so discussed here are responsiveness, continuity, community, and constructive activity. They encapsulate much of what has been discussed in the previous section.

Responsiveness. It is essential to be responsive to the individuality of all adult educators—how they prefer to learn and teach, their prior experience, their evident teaching strengths, and their attitudes to change and innovation adoption. Response to learning and teaching or technology-based application questions or operational problems should be focused and timely.

Continuity. Once-only training sessions for teachers are usually not very effective. Professional development, especially that which is squeezed into already busy schedules, will work best if it is designed as an ongoing, incremental, and cumulative process, a continual cycle of renewal and growth. The Web may be used for slower-paced reflective discussions, real time for faster-paced discussions.

Community. Teachers can grow in their knowledge if nurtured in familiar and helpful communities. It is a good idea to build on the teachers' existing memberships of discipline-based networks to increase the chances of collegial idea sharing. Individuals should be connected across and within the various adopter groups so that each feels grounded and encouraged to keep a balanced outlook. The boundaries of each community can be used to create a safe place to make errors, experiment, complain, tell success stories, and think reflectively. Teachers should also be connected with educational colleagues such as librarians who work closely with learners and course teams.

Constructive Activity. When adult educators are treated like intelligent adult learners, when they are seen by peers and students to be lifelong learners, and when they experience the conditions they plan to create for their own students, then powerful change opportunities emerge. They may focus on real-world tasks and problems, use opportunities for action and reflection and trial and error, take bite-sized chunks in learning a new technology, use the Web in model, moderated discussions, explore and jettison different technology applications, construct their own new knowledge or skills, and question established practice.

Future Directions

Many resources are needed to promote professional development: more stories of reflective practice (Gibson, 2000), advice that is more analytical and reflective than descriptive and prescriptive, and new and interdisciplinary conceptual frames to guide practice. We can use more reminders from the majority adopter groups on how a teacher may best manage her or his interventions in a Web-based course. We can use more analyses of how and why Web use (especially for a course) can be justified in the face of older yet cost-effective, reliable, and efficient learning technologies (O'Rourke, this volume). We need greater proactive involvement from librarians in developing information-literate Web users. Most of all, we need witty, wise, and constructive critiques of all our work on the Web.

References

Barr, R. B., and Tagg, J. "From Teaching to Learning: A New Paradigm for Undergraduate Education." *Change,* 1995, 27(6), 13–25.

Bates, A. W. *Managing Technological Change: Strategies for College and University Leaders.* San Francisco: Jossey-Bass, 1999.

Burge, E. J. "Using Learning Technologies: Ideas for Keeping One's Balance." *Educational Technology,* 1999, 39(6), 45–49.

Cahoon, B. (ed.) *Adult Learning and the Internet.* New Directions for Adult and Continuing Education, no. 78. San Francisco: Jossey-Bass, 1998.

Donovan, M. "Rethinking Faculty Support." *Technology Source,* Sept.-Oct. 1999. [http://horizon.unc.edu/TS/development/1999–09.asp]

Evans, T., and Nation, D. (eds.), *Changing University Teaching: Reflections on Creating Educational Technologies.* London: Kogan Page, 2000.

Fox, R., and Herrmann, A. "Changing Media, Changing Times: Coping with Adopting New Educational Technologies." In T. Evans and D. Nation (eds.), *Changing University Teaching: Reflections on Creating Educational Technologies.* London: Kogan Page, 2000.

Frayer, D. "Creating a Campus Culture to Support a Teaching and Learning Revolution." *CAUSE/EFFECT,* 1999, 22(2). [http://www.educause.edu/ir/library/html/cem0023.html]

Gibson, C. C. "The Ultimate Disorientating Dilemma: The Online Learning Community." In T. Evans and D. Nation (eds.), *Changing University Teaching: Reflections on Creating Educational Technologies.* London: Kogan Page, 2000.

Gillespie, K. H. (ed.). *The Impact of Technology on Faculty Development, Life, and Work.* New Directions for Teaching and Learning, no. 76. San Francisco: Jossey-Bass, 1998.

Holt, M. E. "Ethical Considerations in Internet-Based Adult Education." In B. Cahoon (ed.), *Adult Learning and the Internet.* New Directions for Adult and Continuing Education, no. 78. San Francisco: Jossey-Bass, 1998.

Jonassen, D. H. "Designing Constructivist Learning Environments." In C. M. Reigeluth (ed.), *Instructional Design Theories and Models,* Vol. II. Hillsdale, N.J.: Erlbaum, 1999.

Katz, R. N., and Rudy, J. A. (eds.). *Information Technology in Higher Education: Assessing Its Impact and Planning for the Future.* New Directions for Institutional Research, no. 102. San Francisco: Jossey-Bass, 1999.

Khaslavsky, J., and Shedroff, N. "Understanding the Seductive Experience." *Communications of the ACM,* 1999, 42(5), 45–49.

Latchem, C., and Lockwood, F. (eds.). *Staff Development in Open and Flexible Learning.* London and New York: Routledge, 1998.

Latchem, C., and Moran, L. "Staff Development Issues in Dual-Mode Institutions: The Australian Experience." In C. Latchem and F. Lockwood (eds.), *Staff Development in Open and Flexible Learning.* London: Routledge, 1998.

Oblinger, D. G., and Rush, S. C. *The Learning Revolution: The Challenge of Information Technology in the Academy.* Boston: Anker, 1997.

Prendergast, G. A. "Creating Effective Online Collaborative Educators." In A. Asensio, J. Foster, V. Hodgson, and D. McConnell (eds.), *Networked Learning: Innovative Approaches to Lifelong Learning and Higher Education Through the Internet.* Lancaster-Sheffield: Lancaster University and University of Sheffield, 2000.

Rogers, E. *Diffusion of Innovations* (4th ed.). New York: Free Press, 1995.

Salmon, G. *E-Moderating: The Key to Teaching and Learning Online.* London: Kogan Page, 2000.

Thompson, D. "From Marginal to Mainstream: Critical Issues in the Adoption of Information Technologies for Tertiary Teaching and Learning." In A. Tait and R. Mills (eds.), *The Convergence of Distance and Conventional Education: Patterns of Flexibility for the Individual Learner.* London: Routledge, 1999.

Tickner, S. "Staff Development for Networked Distance Education." In A. Asensio, J. Foster, V. Hodgson, and D. McConnell (eds.), *Networked Learning: Innovative*

Approaches to Lifelong Learning and Higher Education Through the Internet. Lancaster-Sheffield: Lancaster University and University of Sheffield, 2000.

Wills, S., and Alexander, S. "Managing the Introduction of Technology in Teaching and Learning." In T. Evans and D. Nation (eds.), *Changing University Teaching: Reflections on Creating Educational Technologies.* London: Kogan Page, 2000.

Young, J. R. "David Noble's Battle to Defend the 'Sacred Space' of the Classroom." *Chronicle of Higher Education,* Mar. 31, 2000, pp. A47–49.

GENEVIEVE M. GALLANT is instructional designer and project manager at the Open Learning and Information Network, Newfoundland, Canada.

8

The underlying principles of learning and cognition are the same for all media and learning environments, including the Web. Effective learning can happen on the Web if a few key principles of information design and learner guidance are applied.

Constructivist Learning on the Web

Brent Wilson, May Lowry

The World Wide Web is the second major wave of the digital revolution that began with the advent of the personal computer in the 1980s. Like many technologies, the Web brings into being the ideas of early innovators—in this case, ideas about hypertext and universal sharing of documents and texts. But the Web can also be a vehicle for realizing the vision of educational thinkers like Dewey, Piaget, and Vygotsky, who long ago advocated a constructivist or meaning-centered approach to learning and teaching. Constructivism, which stands in contrast to mechanical conceptions of thinking and action, emphasizes the learner's role in constructing meaning—as opposed to simple transmission from teacher to student (Duffy and Cunningham, 1996). Learners do more than process information—they build an understanding through interaction with their environment. Recently, some educators have seized upon computers and the Web as a means of realizing that constructivist ideal—the computer because of its number crunching and data-presentation capabilities, the Web because of its connective and communicative resources.

A number of metaphors have been used to describe the Web: *information highway, digital library, cyberspace,* and *global village.* All are compatible with learners constructing meaning through self-directed inquiry, guided activity, or community-based co-participation. The term *web* itself suggests a vast, complex network of interrelated strands, forming a resilient fabric made strong by the densely interweaving threads, not by any individual end point. Because of its uniquely distributed nature, the Web continues to be seen as a stimulus to innovation, placing more control in the hands of individuals, work groups, and people with shared interests and goals (Brown, 2000).

Yet the Web is a young and immature technology. It is frustratingly slow, often unreliable in content and access, chaotic, with content increasingly dominated by commercial interests. The hype exceeds the reality, and will probably continue to do so for a while. It is even possible that the Web is *meant* to be messy and chaotic, and always will be. But it is the marriage of the technology's raw potential with exciting ideas for learning that generates such keen interest among educational innovators. As we move from promising potential to proven practices, a key question remains: After all the hype, where is the constructivist vision really found on the Web?

Here we look at how the Web can be used to help adults build meaningful understandings and competencies. Our stance is colored by our professional experience as learning designers, but we want to explore how adult learners themselves can make use of the vast resources available on the Web. We hope to show, as our title asserts, that people use the Web all the time for self-directed purposes. The best way to understand the Web's power is by appreciating how people constantly construct meaning through its use.

What Is Constructivism?

Constructivism is one of those slippery words—one that pops up often, but whose meaning is often taken for granted. Rather than consulting a dictionary, we can go to the Web for a definition. A Lycos search shows more than twenty-three thousand hits on the term! Most look like academic sites, although a few commercial sites show up. Our own research site, *IT Connections* (http://www.cudenver.edu/~mryder/itc_data/constructivism.html, maintained by colleague Martin Ryder), is the first recommended link. We go there, and true to the Web, we see nothing but further links. We shoot off to the first link and see a clear description that conveys the basic idea—learners "construct their own knowledge," often with help from a teacher-coach or guide. The second link is dead, but the third link offers a very similar notion: "Constructivists view learning as the result of mental construction. Students learn by fitting new information together with what they already know. People learn best when they actively construct their own understanding" (http://hagar.up.ac.za/catts/learner/lindavr/lindapg1.htm, March 22, 2000). Also provided at this site are bulleted lists of attributes, key words, and phrases. All of these resources help convey a good solid idea about constructivism.

In many ways, our search for a definition illustrates many key features of the Web as a learning resource:

- The Web is a fairly powerful source of information, especially valuable to self-directed learners. Cognitive approaches to learning give emphasis to information processing. The Web is a rich source of information to be processed and understood.
- Some places provide detail, others provide comparison or synthesis. The Web accommodates different purposes—sometimes to show the "big picture," other times to find very specific information.

- Content and links are both valuable. *IT Connections* provides nothing but well-organized links. This can be as valuable as a highly interactive, multimedia site.
- Commerce is mixed in with academia. People approach the Web with different interests, including profit-making and market interests. When reviewing Web resources, users should always ask about motives: Why is this material up here? Who wants me to use this resource, or believe its contents?
- The Web accommodates considerable variability in answers and perspectives. The idea of a single, authoritative answer is hard to reconcile with the multiple, competing voices on the Web. Although it contains massive information like an encyclopedia, the Web as a whole is unedited, not refereed, and always changing.
- Judging content is a critical task the user cannot easily delegate. Users of the Web quickly learn they must judge the quality of conflicting sources. This requires our best reasoning that draws on pertinent background knowledge—along with specific information-literacy skills for interpreting and evaluating information (Hancock, 1993; Kerka, this volume).
- Following links is an important way to learn on the Web. In any reading situation, author and reader share the load of constructing meaning. Because of its hypertext environment, Web users exercise much more control over the learning experience than listeners of lectures or readers of books (Landow, 1992). Thus a person's individual purposes and goals play a critical role in determining the quality and character of the learning experience—true in any learning situation, but especially so on the Web.

Let us now analyze our exercise from a constructivist point of view.

Where was the meaning being constructed? At every point of inquiry and problem definition. Even during relatively free-form browsing episodes, the reader is an active participant and determiner of next steps. Along the winding road of Web browsing, meaning is continually being constructed.

Did our activity constitute a significant alternative to traditional forms of learning and instruction? Yes and no. Web searching is a significant departure from a simple lecture, but educators have always included inquiry as a part of a course of study. The Web exercise was a lot like browsing library stacks—in some ways a departure from classrooms, but certainly consistent with a venerable tradition of self-directed inquiry.

There seems to be a certain redundancy or awkwardness about the term *constructivist learning*. It is like saying, "active learning" every time you want to say "learning." Learning by its nature seems inherently active and constructed. But that is our point exactly: constructivist learning happens all the time on the Web and in classrooms. Meaning construction is not reserved for high-tech, multimedia, project- or problem-based experiences. It happens all the time as people try to make sense of their environments, and of information presented to them.

We may look at constructivist learning in different ways: To some people, constructivism implies specific learning activities or instructional strategies—for example, case- or project-based learning, working within authentic contexts, and so on (Savery and Duffy, 1996). To others, constructivism is a theory of learning. This theory includes the notion of schemas or mental models, and it emphasizes qualitative changes in understanding based on prior knowledge (Mayer, 1996). To still others, constructivism is an underlying way of thinking that informs teaching decisions and activities but does not imply specific strategies (Wilson, 1997). Teaching from a constructivist viewpoint may include a drill, or a lecture, or a prepared reading assignment without sacrifice of principle. A constructivist would ask, What are the fundamental aims? How is meaning construction best facilitated in this case? Strategies are then placed opportunistically to serve these worthwhile ends.

There are pros and cons to each of these positions, but we favor a deeper view that leaves open choices in method. Any strategy—including problem-, project-, and case-based learning—could result in poor learning if used in the wrong way. Our open stance toward strategies leads us to a similar view of the Web: Web-based learning must be evaluated in the context of its use. No particular type of use is absolutely forbidden; everything depends on surrounding conditions (see Greeno and Middle School Mathematics Projects Group, 1998). As our search exercise illustrates, low-tech, "plain-vanilla" strategies (info searches, browsing links, research projects) can be just as valuable as highly packaged and carefully designed presentations or interactions.

Three Core Principles

Greeno offers what could be a mission statement for constructivist learning: "We need to organize learning environments and activities that include opportunities for acquiring basic skills, knowledge, and conceptual understanding, not as isolated dimensions of intellectual activity, but as contributions to students' development of strong identities as individual learners and as more effective participants in the meaningful social practices of their learning communities in school and elsewhere in their lives" (Greeno and Middle School Mathematics Projects Group, 1998, p. 17).

In other words, learners need to develop individual competence, but within a context of effective participation in groups and communities. Following Greeno, we introduce three core principles for effective use of the Web for learning: provide access to rich sources of information; encourage meaningful interactions with content; and bring people together to challenge, support, or respond to each other. These principles, although hardly unique, provide a simple framework for analyzing how constructivist learning happens on the Web.

Provide Access. The Web is most noted for making information more widely available to people. A frequent first thought about a topic is, "I wonder if it's on the Web." The example used in the earlier search exercise used the *IT Connections* Web site to find information about constructivism. The homepage includes a title, an e-mail link to the Web master, a search box, and twelve categories covering research, literature, and discussion opportunities. The simplicity of the page is deceiving, however. Following the first link—"theory and philosophy," for example—takes us to a new series of seventeen linked topics. The scope of theories included is broad, but we can detect from the range of topics that theory and philosophy deals with cognition, culture, and technology. Clicking on the "constructivism" link leads to a two-page list of resources, beginning with ten links to definitions; then an alphabetized list of more than twenty papers; then specific links on Dewey, Piaget, and Vygotsky; then a list of corollary sites. And remember— we are following just one set of links; the site contains hundreds of additional links organized in this fashion. Adult learners with research interests in the areas of cognition, culture, and technology will likely find these links very valuable.

Depending on learning preferences and background knowledge, some people will find a list of links like this overwhelming. Too many links, not enough illustrations or guidance! Other information-seekers, however, can spend hours exploring a rich set of links. These learners can learn more effectively from well-organized links than from an introductory lecture or textbook reading. Although some learners will lack the metacognitive skill and self-defined objectives, many others will find resources like *IT Connections* to be treasure troves of exploration and inquiry.

Here are some additional sites that offer high-quality information:

- *Examples of the Web used for learning* (http://www.mcli.dist.maricopa. edu/tl/about.html). Maricopa Community College in Arizona has a well-earned reputation in the United States for learning innovations. This Web site presents more than seven hundred examples of the Web being used for learning. It serves as a minibrowsing environment with some quality screening, but lots of room to explore. Similar sites are found at the World Lecture Hall (http://www.utexas.edu/world/lecture/); the Blue Web'n collection of Blue Ribbon learning sites (http://www.kn.pacbell.com/wired/bluewebn/); and the Telecampus directory of online courses (http://courses.telecampus.edu/). All of these sites are valuable for what they collect; that is, their links, rather than the new content they present. Here is a notable feature: juxtaposed links serve to make information more accessible, but they also help users synthesize or compare diverse information sources.
- *Top tips for increasing online interactivity* (http://www.learnscope.anta. gov.au/display_stories/1-90000/1501-1800/display_stories_1660.html). The Australian National Training Authority reports thirteen practical tips distilled from an online game hosted by a worldwide conference. These tips are drawn straight from experienced practitioners. We have them

bookmarked because of their value for distance education, and as a reminder of how games can generate worthwhile content.

- *Searching the Web efficiently* (http://edweb.sdsu.edu/Courses/EDTEC532/ search.html). Bernie Dodge of San Diego State University created a simple, two-page job aid to help people improve their use of search engines on the Web. Web-using learners can avoid buying (and reading) a book; rather, they can efficiently learn a procedure and a concept by a short procedural form and an explanation.
- *Grabbing graphics* (http://projects.edtech.sandi.net/staffdev/tpss98/ grabbing_graphics.htm). Web authors know something that not all browsers know: grabbing graphics is very easy to do on the Web. This job aid is very well designed and shows readers exactly how to do it.
- *Guide to business success in Japan* (http://www.anderson.ucla.edu/research/ japan/). This UCLA site provides a number of short, focused guides to doing business in Japan—very similar to "culturegrams" (http://www. culturgram. com/) except that they are Web-based rather than paper-based.

Besides their U.S. origins, what do these examples have in common? All include well-designed presentations of information that could be very useful to the right person. None include high-tech glitz and multimedia, but they easily could if the content warranted. Multimedia can grow on the Web as the technologies develop. The point is that information of all kinds can be placed on the Web and made available for convenient access, bookmarking, and use. A site's value lies partly in the design of the information presented, but remains largely in the hands of the users. When a resource is accessed by a person skilled at self-directed learning and having clear learning goals, then the resource will likely be an effective aid to constructivist learning.

Encourage Meaningful Interactions. Some Web sites guide users through an activity or presentation, thereby encouraging new learning of information, as any teaching resource would do. However, good instruction does more than present information—you get guidance, advice, coaching, feedback (Merrill, 1991). These four features we are more likely to find in well-designed computer-based instruction than on the Web. This is especially apparent when learners use the Web independently, without teacher involvement. The following examples provide good levels of guidance and prompting, but not all sites include high levels of task-specific interactivity and feedback.

- *Higher-Ed Webquest* (http://edweb.sdsu.edu/Courses/ED810/wq3.htm). This Webquest, developed by Allison Rossett and Jim Marshall for a doctoral seminar in educational technology, poses a problem and then directs learners through a set of activities that address the problem. Webquests are guided Web activities following a structure similar to that described earlier (see http://edweb.sdsu.edu/webquest/webquest.html). They constitute a pleasant compromise between open inquiry and controlled instruction, appropriate for the Web.

- Another good Webquest is *Guess Who's Coming to Dinner: A French Rev-olutionary Dining Experience* (http://www.lubbock.k12.tx.us/quests/FrenchRevWebQuest/). Learners prepare to assume the identities of one of four people (King Louis XVI, Marie Antoinette, Rousseau, or Robes-pierre) and then prepare for dinnertime conversation. The site includes instructions for the activity as well as links to help learners research their chosen character.
- *What Is Really True? A Lesson on Constructivism* (http://itech1.coe.uga.edu/faculty/lprieber/constructlesson.html). This little teaching module on constructivism is designed by Lloyd Rieber, University of Georgia. The lesson begins with an audio clip from the U.S. film *A Few Good Men,* in which one actor angrily tells another, "You can't handle the truth!" The movie tie-in and audio clip provide an inviting hook to learn more about constructivism, and the structuring and guidance of this short lesson adds value to the information, helping Web users learn content in a more tar-geted way.

All these sites differ from simple information sites by their teaching features—guided activities, interactions, and feedback. Adult learners lose some flexibility by the added structure, but they gain some additional pro-cessing of information that can lead to solid understanding of the mater-ial. Resources that help learners build meaningful understandings of difficult material are valued in a constructivist perspective.

Bring People Together. When faced with a formidable learning chal-lenge, many learners turn to other people for help. We all think of ourselves in terms of groups we belong to, and very often we set out to learn new material in order to keep up with certain groups or qualify for entry into others. People provide scaffolding, encouragement, and support for our learning forays. They provide alternative perspectives on material. Many constructivist theorists call attention to the social and cultural aspects of meaning construction (for example, Resnick, Levine, and Teasley, 1991). We believe the Web will increase its value as a learning resource to the extent that it can bring people together rather than isolate them.

There is significant loss of information between face-to-face commu-nication and virtual communication. While acknowledging the serious lim-itations of online communication, we believe that some actions are afforded online that are not easily accomplished face-to-face—for example, check-ing your e-mail at a convenient time rather than answering the doorbell upon demand. Although it is still too early to assess this potential of the Web fully, we mention here a few sites that serve to bring people together through collaborative work, discussion, and common interests:

- *Learning design case studies* (http://curry.edschool.virginia.edu/go/ITcases/). For three years running, Mabel Kinzie and students at the University of Virginia hosted a competition open to students in instructional design throughout the world. Each year a new, complex, well-mediated case study was presented online, requiring collaborative problem solving and written response from student teams. A process involving proctors and judges was established to respond to and judge team solutions. All team responses were published to allow further comparison and discussion among participants. Our students participated in these competitions and benefited from the realistic case studies and the cross-program participation. The case studies remain a valuable instructional resource.

- *ITForum, a listserv for instructional-technology professionals* (http://itech1. coe.uga.edu/ITForum/home.html). Subscribers discuss a short contributed paper about once a month. The list discussion has become a staple of Brent Wilson's daily professional life. Over the past five years or so, the archive of papers has become a valuable source of thinking and scholarship related to instructional technology—not quite the consistent quality of a peer-reviewed journal, but more diverse and often more relevant. In addition to paper discussions, the list provides a public forum for discussing professional issues. It also is a popular place to get answers to practical questions that arise in one's work. Discussion groups like ITForum are one of the strengths of the Web, and illustrate the capacity to bring people together to learn (see Wilson and Ryder, 1996, for more discussion of listserv groups as learning communities).
- *Corporate University Exchange, Inc.* (http://www.corpu.com/). This site is nearly a complete Web portal, with links to bookstore, consulting services, conferences and workshops, and bulletin board—in short, just about everything related to corporate universities. Note also its commercial character: commerce gets mixed in with learning goals all the time; the same is true on the Web. The discussions at a site like this depend on a shared interest to sustain their interactions.
- *Click2Learn.com's E-learning portal* (http://www.click2learn.com/ c2l/). Click2Learn.com sponsors another Web portal, this time devoted to learning and career development in the information technology industries. Links are provided to online courses, learning resources, service providers, discussion lists, and chat rooms on a wide variety of IT topics. Again, people come together in a limited way in the context of a commercial venture directed at very targeted learning competencies.

Future Directions

The tone of this chapter has been optimistic and affirmative: the Web is indeed a place where constructivist learning happens all the time. Even so, we do not wish to leave the impression that Web use is without its problems. Learning impasses often happen on the Web—for example, there are broken links, fussy technology, untrustworthy content, slow speeds, and English language bias. Moreover, Web activity may not match every learner's cognitive style or preference.

These difficulties, however, are not reason enough to avoid using a resource. Web users need encouragement to solve their own problems and overcome whatever barriers they encounter—a worthy constructivist goal in itself (Wolin and Wolin, 1993). Future efforts will surely focus on helping users acquire needed skills to manage their own learning on the Web.

At the same time, designers of Web resources are working to adapt learning resources to the needs of individual learners. For example, the learning objects movement (Farance and Tonkel, 1999) seeks to standardize the indexing of media elements (video and audio clips, text segments, and so on) to allow extemporaneous assembly of learning experiences.

Some barriers are not easily overcome by the best efforts of users and designers. Limited access, lack of assistive technologies, or resources designed for exclusive or commercial interests are larger ethical issues to be addressed before the Web can become effectively a universal resource. These limitations also underscore the need to fit Web use into a larger matrix of learning activity.

The future of the Web's impact on learning will hinge on three levels of use—individual, classroom or work group, and societal or cultural. The Web will continue to support constructivist learning as people develop the habit of turning to the Web to solve learning problems. Classrooms and work groups need effective access and opportunities to publish their own work and contribute to the Web's content base. The cumulative effect of individuals and group practices begins to change a culture. In the last ten years, we have only glimpsed the cultural changes at work through the Web and related global exchanges.

We do know that the Web, as a major breakthrough innovation, is here to stay. It is already a significant tool for learning—for those who have access to it and can make use of it. Our best hope is that we adopt the Web appropriately into our everyday learning pursuits as we actively seek to make sense of our worlds.

References

Brown, J. S. "Growing Up Digital: How the Web Changes Work, Education, and the Ways People Learn." *Change,* 2000, 32(2), 11–20.

Duffy, T. M., and Cunningham, D. J. "Constructivism: Implications for the Design and Delivery of Instruction." In D. H. Jonassen (ed.), *Handbook of Research for Educational Communications and Technology.* New York: Macmillan, 1996.

Farance, F., and Tonkel, J. "LTSA Specification: Learning Technology Systems Architecture, Draft 5." (1999, December). Available: http://edutool.com/ltsa May 16, 2000.

Greeno, J. G., and the Middle School Mathematics Through Applications Projects Group. "The Situativity of Knowing, Learning, and Research." *American Psychologist,* 1998, 53(1), 5–26.

Hancock, V. E. "Information Literacy for Lifelong Learning." (ED 358 870) (1993, May). available: http://www.ed.gov/databases/ERIC_Digests/ed358870.html

Landow, G. *Hypertext: The Convergence of Contemporary Critical Theory and Technology.* Baltimore: Johns Hopkins University Press, 1992.

Mayer, R. E. "Learners as Information Processors: Legacies and Limitations of Educational Psychology's Second Metaphor." *Educational Psychologist,* 1996, *31*(3/4), 151–161.

Merrill, M. D. "Constructivism and Instructional Design." *Educational Technology,* 1991, *31*(5), 45–53.

Resnick, L., Levine, J. M., and Teasley, S. D. (eds.). *Perspectives on Socially Shared Cognition.* Washington, D.C.: American Psychological Association, 1991.

Savery, J. R., and Duffy, T. M. "Problem-Based Learning: An Instructional Model and Its Constructivist Framework." In B. G. Wilson (ed.), *Constructivist Learning Environments: Case Studies in Instructional Design* (pp. 135–148). Englewood Cliffs, N.J.: Educational Technology Publications, 1996.

Wilson, B. G. "Reflections on Constructivism and Instructional Design." In C. R. Dills and A. J. Romoszowski (eds.), *Instructional Development Paradigms* (pp. 63–80). Englewood Cliffs, N.J.: Educational Technology Publications, 1997.

Wilson, B., and Ryder, M. "Dynamic Learning Communities: An Alternative to Designed Instruction." In M. Simonson (ed.), *Proceedings of Selected Research and Development Presentations* (pp. 800–809). Washington, D.C.: Association for Educational Communications and Technology, 1996.

Wolin, S., and Wolin, S. *The Resilient Self.* New York: Villiard Books, 1993.

BRENT WILSON (*http://www.cudenver.edu/~bwilson*) *and* MAY LOWRY (*may_lowry@ceo.cudenver.edu*) *are both professors of information and learning technologies, University of Colorado at Denver.*

9

Highlighted concepts from each chapter create a holistic framework for reflective and strategic thinking about learning technologies.

Synthesis: Learners and Learning Are the Issues

Elizabeth J. Burge

It is time now to synthesize the reflective and strategic thinking found in the earlier chapters. Like you, I am a naturally constructivist learner; that is, my brain is "wired" to construct my own meanings from my interactions with the authors' and my own experience. So what you now read shows the result so far of my sense-making of the eight preceding chapters. It is not an exhaustive or objective analysis: a word limit applies and my personal and professional values influence my choices. The somewhat conversational style of this chapter is influenced by Jennifer O'Rourke's reminder in Chapter Five to use print as a one-on-one, connected communication tool rather than a one-to-many, disconnected display of knowledge. As I reflected on each chapter, I selected one or two short quotations to serve as an *aide memoire,* to give me concepts concise enough for easy recall later. No doubt by now you have chosen some too.

The synthesis has three parts: my selection of key ideas made by each author—those frank and useful reflections on practice that trigger my own reflections; highlights from the strategic thinking in this book; and finally some questions, because as the legendary Canadian literature scholar Northrop Frye once said, "There are no answers, only more questions."

Reflective Thinking

"Trigger intrinsic motivation" and *"use technology to cue and support cognitive strategies."* When an adult learner's motivating drives of competence and connectedness, or achievement and affiliation (MacKeracher, 1996) are not engaged by the conditions in the learning environment, then the

learner is in trouble and the educator somewhat blind to what is needed. Rather than asking "How do I motivate a learner?" it is more appropriate to ask "What am I or others doing that is blocking the learner's intrinsic motivating drives?" Christine Olgren's own use of technology to cue and support thinking helps keep my attention on what should be happening inside the learner's head and how those information-processing activities may be helped and hindered by the learner and by various environmental conditions. Technology to her is a factor in an environment that needs to be "landscaped" by her deliberate use of the whole repertoire of learning strategies. Adult learners will do their own landscaping too, as they explained recently and rather frankly while describing their mixed reactions to using four conferencing technologies (Office of Learning Technologies, 1998). Educators of adults are not much different, as their stories can show (Haughey and Anderson, 1998).

"*(Learners) want whatever works best for them.*" "*Ignoring the new learning technologies is not an option, but . . . use them appropriately alongside traditional teaching and learning media.*" Marion Phillips and Patrick Kelly raised issues that made me think again about that often-used term: *learner support.* "A crutch, as in a deficit model?" I asked them from my own experience of exchanging study problems and achievements with adult learners. On that question now hangs a story of lively collegial discussion and critical self-awareness, and you have seen the end result: learner service. Such service encompasses all the dimensions of the complex process of helping adult learners manage all their learning environments—at home, in paid and unpaid work settings, or as part of a formal educational institution. In ordinary life roles, adults want and need to feel in control and able to secure "just-in-time" (that is, timely, and not "just-in-case") help, so these principles apply to educators too. "Whatever works best for them" is a real challenge to educators who, understandably, may tend to plan their version of what is needed. Being relevant to learners is also a challenge for many technology-oriented administrators who see marketing advantage in using the latest technology. As Marion and Patrick reminded me, what is more important in the long view is the extent to which any learner service earns the loyalty of those learners over their learning lifespan. As they illustrate without saying it, they and their colleagues have designed more of a holistic technology—one that leaves the doer in total control of the process—rather than a prescriptive technology—one that is designed to produce total user compliance and conformity (see the now classic distinction by Franklin, 1999).

"*We need to focus more attention on the 'why' and 'for what purpose' as . . . we rethink the notion of literacy.*" Sandra Kerka's emphasis on learners having the skills of information literacy and critical thinking links to Christine Olgren's discussion of a capable adult learner and Brent Wilson and May Lowry's discussion of constructing knowledge. Clearly, if I lack the needed literacies to interrogate any information regarding its origin, functions, and biases, I may fall prey to the promises of high-speed and high-volume technologies, or worse still, become disillusioned and grab whatever seems to get me through. Sandra's remit for the chapter excluded the role of the skilled librarian, but there is an enhanced role for these professionals if they can come to where the learners are—literally and metaphorically (Burge and Snow, 2000). As more material on the Web is designed to maximize its hypertext features, many adults will need fast help to orient themselves and reach their destination. Here is another opportunity for information literacy specialists to thrive if they know how to assist adults who cognitively and emotionally may "freeze" when confronted with a torrent of information (when all they needed was a glassful).

"Hindsight is easier to manage than foresight." Yes indeed. Allan Herrmann, Robert Fox, and Anna Boyd helped me to think about how to distinguish unintended effects from professional malpractice and to categorize them into useful groupings. It is not easy to separate the operations of Murphy's Law—in its colloquial form, "Anything that can go wrong, will"— from the often invisible and cumulative effects of evolutionary and adaptive processes contained in the laws of media (McLuhan and McLuhan, 1988). It is worth summarizing them here to help you think about the origins of any technology you use today. As a technology extends our task capabilities somehow (that is, as it acts as a tool), it will also render out of date whatever technology helped us do the task earlier (for example, the computer replaces the typewriter for the production of text). But the new technology may also "retrieve" or render essential some other older technology (paper) and as its development increases to a new limit, will assume changed roles or forms (speech recognition software for text production). Logan (1995) gives other examples from everyday life. In these laws lie many opportunities for anticipating unintended effects. In the intersections between technology change and technology use lie many opportunities for experiencing unintended effects. My personal untested theory is that unintended effects may be minimized if I use some foresight—that is, if I look at any technology designed to assist learning, compare its form and function with earlier forms and functions, and try to anticipate counterintuitive behaviors required by the new technology (for example, the Meekathara or the videoconferencing experiences discussed in Chapter Four).

"To learn from, to learn with, and to learn beside" print. These three functions surely explain *"the durability, portability, and accessibility of print."* I am sure you recognized Jennifer O'Rourke's ease and skill in moving forward so fluidly on the earlier pages. Adult education practitioners of her experience know how to create shape, texture, and pacing on the flat immobile surface of paper; and therein lies the sophistication of print as a learning technology. As with audioconferencing, the psychomotor operational skills pale into insignificance compared with the cognitive and affective skills required for the design of information presentation and stimulation of dialogue about it (Hartley, 1996). As with any other technology, print carries the conflicts of opposing qualities: its durability in

book or bound form inhibits frequent changes, and its inscribed "authority" as presenter of knowledge may lead readers into an uncritical acceptance. One implication of this chapter, if we take seriously the two competence and connectedness motivating drives of adults, is how to enhance those drives using a text-form presence. Because we authors wanted you to use this book as a "presenter," as a "companion," and as an "extension" of ourselves as people, we had to work hard at achieving a connectedness with you without lapsing into undue familiarity. It is a delicate task, because we have no feedback from you as we write.

"Whether radio is received as background or foreground depends on the choice of the listener." "The human voice creates a powerful presence." May Maskow shows the power of perception here. Radio may be a ubiquitous technology, but like print it has not consistently been treated with the attention it needs to function as a higher-profile effective learning technology. Radio producers make their own decisions about whether their program should be heard as background while the adult's attention is fully focused on a complex or new task (searching the Internet) or as foreground when the adult's task requires no conscious or sustained attention (walking). But learners will cheerfully and efficiently decide for themselves, just as during the audioconferenced delivery of what a teacher thinks are pearls of wisdom a group of adults at another site will turn such audio down or off in order to create their own acoustic space for discussing topics they deem as more important! Salutary information, that. Good audio broadcasts and recordings can reach into one's heart and mind in a way that very few other media can. For example, Alastair Cooke's "Letter from America" radio broadcasts were masterful expressions of text written for the ear; for me as a young listener in Australia many years ago, they acted like theaters for my exploring mind. Such goodness—that is, fitness for purpose and fitness for medium—comes with skill, but many educators and learners (in my experience) have never been helped to consider how the qualities of their voice influence the effect of their presence in a learning community. As May illustrates, given the effects of well-modulated voices speaking engagingly to a single adult listener, radio is not the medium for sending out solo-voiced lectures, even if the talker has been trained professionally. Even if the voice quality alone does not provoke the "off" response, the listener's attention span may nevertheless stimulate a mental signal of boredom and the lecturer will be eased into the background—not what was intended! If radio is to enjoy a renaissance based on the laws of media (McLuhan and McLuhan, 1988), we adult learners and educators have to consider how to link the features of the medium with the repertoire of learning strategies and how radio may reinvent itself.

"It becomes quite a challenge for some of them to shift gears or indeed change vehicles and adopt other models." Genevieve Gallant identifies a challenge and a process for many thoughtful educators as their confrontation with a technology sends them off to examine the relevance of their inher-

ited teaching model. The same issue applies with learners, of course, in adapting or changing their models of learning, but that is another story. Unspoken anxieties have an impact too: fear of the unknown, potential loss of status with learners or prestige with peers, management of increased workload, and loss of academic rigor if new ways of teaching are linked to hot new technologies. A skilled professional developer will be able to sense the adopter category most relevant to each educator as well as identify that person's current teaching strengths and development areas and use them to guide further development. For example, Mellon's (1999) reflections on technologies for learning and teaching are a prime example of the balanced, reflective thinking of a mature "majority" category practitioner who is not distracted from the fundamentals of good teaching (Haag, 1992). Wise, energy-efficient professional developers will manage their energy levels so that they can give enough attention later to the majority adopters, rather than exhausting themselves on the change-chasing early adopters (Brittmarie Myringer, personal communication, May 2000).

The educator can sometimes best be helped by experiencing the conditions he or she intends to set up for the learners—for example, taking a course on the Web or listening to one's own PowerPoint presentation. There is now a new weariness syndrome to manage—"PowerPoint fatigue" as I have heard it called—but the problem here is how the technology has been used, not the technology itself. Although such awareness exercises are useful, they may not always help developing trainers or teachers see either how they unwittingly impose their own learning style preferences on the learners or why they reject a particular learning technology. An example: a face-to-face teacher rejects audio- or computer conferencing because he needs to "see the whites of their eyes." What is the essential problem here? Again, technology is not the key problem; it appears more to be a control issue, and visibility of adult learners should not be a condition for control, however defined. Ways can be found to compensate for the loss of certain paralinguistic cues, as the use of the so-called emoticons on computer screens demonstrates. Genevieve's chapter keeps the focus on the primacy of people before technology.

"Constructivist learning happens all the time." "As we try to move from promising potential to proven practice." Brent Wilson and May Lowry show how we try to make our own sense of the world regardless of what educators do and not do. So if it is a natural tendency, why don't we see more of it, and less of the transmission of predigested information? I provoke you; I'm sure you know the answer. But seriously, is it mainly because some teachers of adults may feel bereft if they give up their visible status or control of talktime and rely instead on other forms of relevance? That question aside, Brent and May alerted me to several points needing more thought. They are that links to other functional Web sites are, generically speaking, as important as the content in each one; that the torrent versus glassful of information problem is still a big one; that people will be people and rely on those they know and trust for information; and that a Web site has to earn its continuing importance for a learner. Learning style preferences (Keefe, 1988) influence a learner's reactions to all those hypertext-filled screens—some will be energized by the foraging strategies required and serendipitous results gained, whereas others will look for some imposed structure because they cannot tolerate such apparent chaos. The movement from promising potential to proven practice happens incrementally and experientially over time, as mature practitioners know. So avoid feeling pressured to conform to what is fashionable: there will always be new technologies, but there is never a guarantee of enough wise and publicly articulate adult and continuing educators.

Strategic Thinking

Although this volume could not accommodate every learning technology currently available, you may agree with me that there must be some strategic thinking that could be applied to any learning technology. Here is my choice, based on what I found in the chapters and my own practitioner experience, and synthesized into eleven themes to reduce your information load:

- *Ownership:* of learning by learners and teaching by teachers, and of technology mistakes as learning opportunities
- *Reality checks:* of which technologies learners can actually access, of the reliability of any technology, of who controls institutional technology budgets, of how learners and educators actually construct their understandings about learning and about learning technologies, and of any unintended effects emerging from intentional practice
- *Self-assessment:* of values, learning needs, and current habits as an educator of adults
- *Legitimation:* of learners' and educators' own perceptions of their words and goals
- *Responsibilities:* differentiated and clarified between project partners, and between learners and teachers or tutors
- *Development:* of people first, second, and third; technology later
- *Access:* on user's terms as far as possible, to learner services, to appropriately competent teachers, librarians
- *Advisers:* well-designed resources in all formats, peer learning groups, and "safe" spaces for learning (be they acoustic, physical, or virtual)
- *Diversity:* of information presentation forms, of learning activities, of interaction voices
- *Critical questioning:* about why any learning technology may be deemed either essential or useful, and how it may mix with other deliberate choices
- *Elegance:* in any technology application that optimizes intrinsic human drives (such as competence and connectedness), optimizes its own best features, and helps a learner and teacher work effectively toward intended outcomes—with the minimum of user effort

Questions for the Future

So far, and depending on how your learning style preferences operate, you have heard or seen or felt, with varying degrees of tolerance, many ideas from all of us authors. Now it is time for us to fade into the background and give you more space for your own reflective and strategic thinking. How to do this? You will have your own ways, and one is asking yourself creative or out-of-the-box questions (or as my students express it—"Liz's brain-burning questions"). Here are some that occur to me as I take my leave and thank you for being part of our dialogue in this book: (1) How do I now think about the concept of learning technologies? If any metaphors are involved, how do they illuminate my constructions of reality? (2) Ethics: What does it mean to be an ethical user of any learning technology? (3) Walking my talk with learning technologies: Where are the difficulties in being congruent? (4) What, in general terms, does it take for an adult learner to act with competence and feel connected in a technologically mediated learning environment?

There are no answers, only more questions. . . .

References

Burge, E. J., and Snow, J. E. "Candles, Corks, and Contracts: Essential Relationships Between Learners and Librarians." *The New Review of Libraries and Lifelong Learning,* 2000, *1*(1), 19–34.

Franklin, U. *The Real World of Technology* (2nd ed.). Toronto, Ontario: House of Anansi Press, 1999.

Haag, S. "Speaking Personally." *American Journal of Distance Education,* 1992, *6*(3), 72–76.

Hartley, J. "Text Design." In D. H. Jonassen (ed.), *Handbook of Research for Educational Communications and Technology.* New York: Macmillan, 1996.

Haughey, M., and Anderson, T. *Networked Learning: The Pedagogy of the Internet.* Montreal: Cheneliere/McGraw-Hill, 1998.

Keefe, J. A. *Profiling and Using Learning Style.* Reston, Va.: National Association of Secondary School Principals, 1988.

Logan, R. K. *The Fifth Language: Learning a Living in the Computer Age.* Toronto, Ontario: Stoddart, 1995.

MacKeracher, D. *Making Sense of Adult Learning.* Toronto, Ontario: Culture Concepts, 1996.

McLuhan, M., and McLuhan, E. *Laws of the Media: The New Science.* Toronto, Ontario: University of Toronto Press, 1988.

Mellon, C. A. "Technology and the Great Pendulum of Education." *Journal of Research on Computing in Education,* 1999, *32*(1), 28–35.

Office of Learning Technologies. Human Resources Development Canada (OLT/HRDC). *Learning on the Information Highway: A Learner's Guide to the Technologies.* Ottawa, Ontario: OLT/HRDC, 1998. [http://www.RobertsAssoc.on.ca]

ELIZABETH J. BURGE, a guest professor at Mid Sweden University for 2000–2001, is professor of adult education and distance education at the University of New Brunswick in Atlantic Canada.

INDEX

Back Issue/Subscription Order Form

Copy or detach and send to:
Jossey-Bass, 350 Sansome Street, San Francisco CA 94104-1342

Call or fax toll free!
Phone 888-378-2537 6AM-5PM PST; Fax 800-605-2665

Back issues: Please send me the following issues at $23 each.
(Important: please include series initials and issue number, such as ACE78.)

1. ACE _____

_____

_____

$ _____ Total for single issues

$ _____ Shipping charges (for single issues **only;** subscriptions are exempt from shipping charges): Up to $30, add $5^{50} • $30^{01}–$50, add $6^{50} $50^{01}–$75, add $8 • $75^{01}–$100, add $10 • $100^{01}–$150, add $12 Over $150, call for shipping charge.

Subscriptions Please ❑ start ❑ renew my subscription to *New Directions for Adult and Continuing Education* for the year _____ at the following rate:

U.S.:	❑ Individual $58	❑ Institutional $104
Canada:	❑ Individual $83	❑ Institutional $129
All Others:	❑ Individual $88	❑ Institutional $134

NOTE: Subscriptions are quarterly, and are for the calendar year only. Subscriptions begin with the Spring issue of the year indicated above.

$ _____ Total single issues and subscriptions (Add appropriate sales tax for your state for single issues. No sales tax on U.S. subscriptions. Canadian residents, add GST for subscriptions and single issues.)

❑ Payment enclosed (U.S. check or money order only)

❑ VISA, MC, AmEx, Discover Card #_____ Exp. date_____

Signature _____ Day phone _____

❑ Bill me (U.S. institutional orders only. Purchase order required.)

Purchase order #_____

Federal Tax I.D. 135593032   GST 89102-8052

Name _____

Address _____

_____

Phone_____ E-mail _____

For more information about Jossey-Bass, visit our Web site at:
www.josseybass.com   **PRIORITY CODE = ND1**